Young Writers 2005

PLAYGROU

Let your creativity flow...

ode

limerick   haiku

rhyme

balla

My Poems

- Inspirations From Scotland
Vol II
Edited by Jessica Woodbridge

 Young**Writers**

First published in Great Britain in 2005 by:
Young Writers
Remus House
Coltsfoot Drive
Peterborough
PE2 9JX
Telephone: 01733 890066
Website: www.youngwriters.co.uk

SB ISBN 1 84602 236 3

Foreword

Young Writers was established in 1991 and has been passionately devoted to the promotion of reading and writing in children and young adults ever since. The quest continues today. Young Writers remains as committed to the fostering of burgeoning poetic and literary talent as ever.

This year's Young Writers competition has proven as vibrant and dynamic as ever and we are delighted to present a showcase of the best poetry from across the UK. Each poem has been carefully selected from a wealth of *Playground Poets* entries before ultimately being published in this, our thirteenth primary school poetry series.

Once again, we have been supremely impressed by the overall high quality of the entries we have received. The imagination, energy and creativity which has gone into each young writer's entry made choosing the best poems a challenging and often difficult but ultimately hugely rewarding task - the general high standard of the work submitted amply vindicating this opportunity to bring their poetry to a larger appreciative audience.

We sincerely hope you are pleased with our final selection and that you will enjoy *Playground Poets - Inspirations From Scotland Vol II* for many years to come.

Contents

Dominic Stewart (12)   16
Steven Harris (11)   16
Robbie Docherty (11)   17
Jai Frape (11)   17
Craig Spence (11)   18
Nicole Hunter (11)   18
Matthew Childs (12)   19
Lee Thomson (11)   19
Nicole Graham (11)   20

Bankhead Primary School, Rutherglen

Sophie Booth (9)   20
Kirsty Allison (9)   20
Bianca Muir (10)   21
Angela Vincent (9)   21
Chloe Sanders (9)   21
Claire Moore (10)   22
Kim Dornan (9)   22
Josh Mackay (10)   22
Jenna Reid (9)   23
Greg Cowan (9)   23
Graeme Dickie (10)   23
Barry Lawrie (9)   24
Adelle Brown (9)   24
Lauren McPherson (10)   24
Martin Tracey (10)   25
William MacPherson (10)   25
Luke Pye (10)   26
David Stephen (9)   26
Dylan McDermott (9)   26
Jordan McNaught (9)   27
Kerry McNeice (9)   27
Howe Yee Shing (10)   27
Lauren McArthur (11)   28
Nicola Mitchell (8)   28
Gavin Irvine (10)   28
Megan Young (10)   29
Adam Stewart (9)   29
Jay Prentice (9)   29
Craig Dallas (10)   30
Melissa Crabb (10)   30

Ciara Tollan (9)	31
Susanne Shaw (9)	31
Jodie Brannan (8)	32
Jordan Wallace (8)	32
Joshua Hurley (8)	32
Robert Hamilton (8)	33
Jordan McPhee (8)	33
Lisa McPherson (8)	33
Megan Stewart (10)	34
Georgina Ely (10)	34
Lauren McGugan (11)	35
Ashleigh Curran (8)	35
Kirsty Howard (10)	36

Banton Primary School, Glasgow

Gregor Campbell (11)	36
Emma Stewart (11)	36
Rebecca MacAngus (11)	37
Lucy Thomson (10)	37
Megan Adam (11)	37
George Douglas (11)	38
Nicole Cameron (10)	38
Bonnie Cameron (11)	38
Michael McMillan (11)	39
Gemma Gilmour (11)	39
John Paterson (10)	39
Rachel Wilson (10)	40

Burnside Primary School, Rutherglen

| Eve Lucas (11) | 40 |

Craigielea Primary School, Paisley

Josh Weir (10)	41
Neil Carter (10)	41
Stewart Bruce (10)	41
Paige Gilchrist (9)	42
Callum Colvin (10)	42
Robert Larkin (9)	42
Demi Stewart (9)	43
Katie Davidson (9)	43
Jay Stewart (10)	43

Andrew Carter (10)	44
Demi Foulds (10)	44
Alison Burgess (10)	44
Tammi Cameron (10)	45
Lauren Kidd (10)	45
Cameron Thomson (10)	45
Jordan Gemmell (9)	45
Rebecca Bools (9)	46

Duncan Forbes Primary School, Inverness

Chloe Vass (10)	46
Eilidh Campbell (11)	47
Rebecca Waugh (11)	48
Ellen McKenzie (11)	49
Alyssa Cook (11)	50
Hayley Smyth (10)	51
Calum Green (10)	52
Chelsea Bolt (10)	53
Charis Crawford-Mair (11)	54

Fort William RC Primary School, Fort William

Emma Haines (10)	54
Natalie Rosie (10)	55
Jessica MacDonald (11)	55
Calum Davidson Hunter (11)	55
Raymond Munro (10)	56
Taylor Matheson (10)	56
Conor Taylor (10)	56
Nicole Calderwood (10)	57
Louise Alexander (10)	57
Savanah Symmers (9)	57
Keira Matheson (11)	58
Connar Mackay (12)	58

Foulford Primary School, Fife

Shelley Forbes (11)	58
Marnie Elise Taylor (11)	59

Gargunnock Primary School, Stirling

Stewart Leask (7)	59
Adam Clayson (7)	59
Amy Bruce (8)	60
Scott MacArthur (8)	60
Andrew Fitches (8)	60
Colum Blackwood (8)	61
Alistair Petrie (7)	61
Mark Parry (8)	61
Alasdair Hyland (8)	62
Juliet Jones (8)	62
Katherine Lewis (8)	62
Lucas Jones (8)	62
Sam Christie (7)	63

Hopeman Primary School, Hopeman

Sam Ash (8)	63
Ellie Hunnybun (9)	64
Connor Dunn (8)	65
Thomas Collins (8)	66
Ethan Williams (9)	66
Daniel Christie (8)	67
Cara Main (11)	67
Ross Dick (9)	68
Stuart Gray (8)	68
Shannon East (8)	69
Harry Ward (10)	69
Anna McPherson (9)	70
Ashleigh Tripp (8)	71
Lauren Oram (8)	72
Forest Napier (9)	73
Charlotte Ball (9)	74
Sarah Allanson (11)	75
Bethannay Grey (9)	76
Thomas Johnson (10)	77
Kathrin Munday (10)	78
Ailie Robertson (11)	79
Corin Smith (10)	80

Kellands School, Inverurie

Hannah Foubister (8)	80
Clair Binnie (10)	81
Jamie Dow (12)	81
Maia Stanton (9)	82
Harriet Paterson (9)	82
Louise O'Rourke (8)	82
Rosalind Watt (9)	83
Kirstin Mitchell (8)	83
Struan Cruickshank (9)	83
Phillip Woodgreaves (8)	84
David Biddle (9)	84
Jason Banks (8)	84
Ben Rattray (9)	85
Orianne Watt (10)	85
Tony Wishart (9)	85
Sean Mayberry (9)	86
Calum Yule (9)	86

Kildrum Primary School, Cumbernauld

Sarah-Jane Sawdon (8)	86
Sophie Cavanagh (8)	87
Kirsty Deakin (8)	87
Chelsea Tominey (9)	88
Ruth McCutcheon (9)	88
Emma McIntosh (8)	89
Emma Henderson (9)	90
Kayleigh Tominey (9)	91

Kininmonth Primary School, Peterhead

Melanie Robinson (11)	92
Shane McDonald (11)	93
Suzann McDonald (11)	94
Sophie Payne (10)	94
Patterson Gough (11)	95
Jacquie Leel (11)	96
Paul Murray (11)	96
Deon Allen (11)	97
Meggie Gough (10)	97
Alastair Robinson (10)	98
Alexandra Abbott (11)	99

Longforgan Primary School, Longforgan

Louise MacGregor (9)	99
Alexander Hayes (11)	100
Callum Fowlie (11)	101
Caitlin Fowlie (9)	102
Daniel Davidson (9)	102
Melissa Lonie (9)	102
Ray Lynham (9)	103

McGill Primary School, Glasgow

Shannon Shields (10)	103
Stuart Beveridge (11)	104
Dale Carroll (9)	105
Amy Brown (10)	106
Emma McArthur (9)	106
John Chaudhry (11)	107
Rebecca Lees (10)	107
Lisa McLauchlan (11)	108
Daniel Kelly (9)	108
Gavin Docherty (11)	109
Lee McLuckie (11)	110
David Dawson (10)	111
Amy McLachlan (9)	112
Samantha Gorrell (11)	113
Janice Buchanan (10)	114

Mosspark Primary School, Glasgow

Jordan Stewart (9)	115
Jonathan McInulty (7)	115
Maryam Raza (7)	115
Reiss Callaghan (8)	116
Chad Meechan (8)	116
Amy Gow (8)	117
Jacob Collins (8)	117
Lucy Mathieson (8)	118
Gary Hannah (8)	118
Rebecca McIlroy (7)	118

Newcastle Primary School, Glenrothes

Ashley Ross (10)	119
Darren Wallace (12)	119

Joanne Kelly (10)	119
Danielle Sweeney (11)	120
Nadya Glen (12)	120
Kirstie Sinclair (11)	121
Caitlin Collins (11)	121
Andrew Bathie (11)	121
Emma Fotheringham (11)	122
Kirsten Elder (11)	122
Samantha Gibson (11)	122
Craig Hutchison (11)	123
Alastair Wallace (12)	123
Melissa Paul (11)	123
Lauren McLeod (11)	124
Louise Wallace (10)	124
Sarah Mann (11)	124

Our Lady of the Annunciation School, Glasgow

Jack Allison (10)	125
Antony Mellon (9)	125
Anna Kennedy (9)	126
Ryan Gallagher (10)	126
Steven Clark (9)	127
Mark Airlie (10)	127
Melissa McFarlane (10)	128
Adam Cavanagh (10)	128
Paddy Campbell (9)	129
Sean Coyle (8)	129
Michael Dunne (9)	130
James Gallacher (10)	131
Owen Sweeney (9)	132
Patrick Hughes (8)	132
Molly McGovern (8)	133
Paul Grindlay (9)	133
Charlotte Jack (9)	134
Laura Quinn (11)	134
Mairi Benham (9)	135
Scott Donachy (10)	135
Hannah Ruddy (9)	136
Andrew Brown (9)	136
Meghan Hughes (9)	137
David Conkie (8)	137

Rachel Sharp (10)   138
Stuart McGibbon (9)   138
John Carson (11)   139
Jennifer Marley (9)   139
Kathryn Marley (10)   140
Bernadette Campbell (11)   141
Sarah Airlie (12)   142
Lauren McAreavey (8)   142
Ben Moran (11)   143
Gemma West (11)   143
Lucy Middleton (10)   144
Olivia Gough (9)   144
Eve Gordon (10)   145
Balal Saleemi (9)   145
Kamil Demiroz (9)   146
James Forrester (9)   146
Megan Darroch (9)   147
Grace Symes (9)   147
Daniel Milgrew (9)   148
Paul McMahon (10)   148
Luke Robertson (11)   149
Kerry Connolly (11)   149
Martin McLaughlin (10)   150
Steven Benham (10)   150
Jordan Devine (10)   151
Barry Morgan (10)   151
Kelsey Lipton (10)   152
Aidan McKendrick (9)   152
Evlyn Russell (10)   153
Liam Macpherson (9)   153

Richmond Park School, Glasgow
Maram Elfleet (11)   154
Jodie Taylor (11)   154
William Marshall (10)   154
Dean Burrell (11)   155

Rimbleton Primary School, Glenrothes
Josh Moody (8)   155
Amy McKillop (9)   156
Graham McSeveney (8)   156

Liam McKinney (8)	157
Jamie Farmer (8)	158
Katie Walker (8)	158
Connor Currie (9)	159
Yasmine Petrie (8)	159
Deni Latimer (8)	160
Jordan Farrell (9)	160
Samantha Riddell (8)	161
Connor Herd (9)	161
Amy Kirkum (9)	162
Sarah-Jane Brand (9)	162
Kirsty Howard (8)	163
Katie Jenkins (8)	163
Grant Donaldson (9)	164
Troi Scott (9)	164
Rona Hamilton (8)	165
Jade Harper (8)	165
Barry Kerr (8)	166
Megan Cameron (8)	166
Aidan Kirkwood (8)	167

St Angela's Primary School, Glasgow

Jordan Wright (11)	167
Chloé McNamee (12)	167
Courtney Hollis (11)	168
Charlene Lang (11)	168
Gemma Bradley (11)	169
Humza Iqbal (12)	169
Kathleen Shaw (11)	170
Peter Merrick (11)	170
Cuebong Wong (12)	171
Shannon McGregor (11)	171
Emma Hannah (11)	172
Sara Boussouara (11)	173

St Brigid's Primary School, Newmains

James Jackson (8)	174
Aileen McKenna (8)	174
Declan Sinclair (8)	175
Megan Stewart (8)	175
Kelly Weir (9)	176

Conor Higgins (8)	176
Gemma Wilson (8)	177
Sarah Hamilton (8)	177
Barry Gilfillan (8)	178
Kayleigh Weir (8)	178
Martin Morrow (8)	179
Kieran Greig (8)	179
Stephen Donnelly (9)	180
Erin McKenna (8)	180
Nicholas Dow (8)	181
Dean Davis (8)	181
Madeleine Lang (9)	182
Jamie-Lee Kean (8)	183
Brian Jordan (8)	184
Stephen Murray (8)	184
Stephanie Harbison (9)	185
Thomas Clifford (8)	185
Dayna Donaldson (8)	186
Emma Weir (8)	186
Aaron Bradshaw (9)	187
Lily Frame (8)	187
Skye Cutler (8)	188
Declan Lafferty (8)	188
Diarmiad McGarrell (8)	189
Peter Kirley (8)	189

St Margaret's Primary School, Loanhead

Harry Lindsay (6)	190
Michael McCormick (6)	190
Samantha Collier (6)	190
Clare Phillips (6)	191
Eilidh Joyce (6)	191
Daniel Turner (7)	191
Lauren Dalgetty (7)	192
Marie Barry (7)	192
Karen Zhu (7)	192
Lewis Brown (6)	193
Chloe Coombs (7)	193
Theo Koulis (7)	193
Eilidh Ramsay (9)	194
Lyndsay Turner (9)	194

Naa Shika Tetteh-Lartey (9)	194
Katelyn Grant (7)	195
Indya Nisbet (7)	195
Tanisha Buerle (7)	195
Sheryl Cochrane (8)	196
John Weir (8)	196
Yasmin Crosbie (8)	196
Robbie Forbes (11)	197
Lewis Crosbie (10)	197
Brooke McGuinness (11)	197
Paul Darcy (8)	198
Benjamin Aarhus (9)	198
William Anderson (10)	198
Emily Dalgetty (7)	199
Raymond Brumby (12)	199
Simon McCormick (9)	199
Ryan Crosbie (12)	200

Sandhaven Primary School, Sandhaven

Chelsea Meadows (10)	200
Kyle Davis (10)	201
Stephanie Smith (10)	201
Megan Beedie (10)	202
Jason Milne (10)	203
Jade Davis (11)	204
Heather Stewart (11)	205
Skye Thompson (11)	206
Martin-Andrew Duncan (10)	207
Caroline Russell (11)	208
Keir Allan (10)	208
Johnathan Beedie (10)	209
Andrew Smith (10)	209
Terri-Lee Batty (11)	210

The Poems

Silence

Silence is a mouse
scurrying along the ground.

Silence is a ballerina dancing on a stage.

Silence is at 12.30 on Christmas Eve
when everyone is sleeping.

Silence is an owl flying through the sky.

Silence is in a boat out at sea
when the water is calm.

Silence is in space; far, far away.

Jade Millar (11)
Aberhill Primary School, Fife

Silence

Silence is white
like a blank page.

Silence is like seeing snow
falling on a cold day.

Silence is like being
in an abandoned house.

Silence is the sound
of a triangle going *bing!*

Silence is a rabbit eating leaves.
Silence is when everyone is sleeping.

Samantha Fraser (9)
Aberhill Primary School, Fife

Snow

If I was snow
I would be as white
as a cloud.

If I was snow
I would look like a sheep.

If I was snow
I would sound like ice.

If I was snow
I would feel as cold
as water.

Chloe Kennedy (9)
Aberhill Primary School, Fife

Silence

Silence is blue.

Silence is when
the day is getting old.

Silence is when
a deer runs through the grass.

Silence is in the field.
Silence is when my mum is sleeping

And when it is silent, I feel lonely.

Donald Davies (11)
Aberhill Primary School, Fife

Anger

Anger is deep red.

It tastes like pepper and onion
and it smells like burning fire.

It sounds like something
terrible has happened

and it feels like
a rough carpet.

When I am angry,
I feel annoyed.

Emma Rodger (10)
Aberhill Primary School, Fife

Silence

Silence is purple.
Silence is at night.

Silence is like being
on my own at the beach.

Silence is like a rat
scuttling about.

Silence is the sound
of the sea.

Ryan Thomson (9)
Aberhill Primary School, Fife

Snow

If I were snow
I would be as white
as vanilla ice cream.

If I was snow
I would taste like salt.

If I was snow
I would sound
like a pin dropping.

Shaun Irvine (9)
Aberhill Primary School, Fife

Good Holidays

I'm going on my holidays
To the seaside to have fun
I am excited to go there
And I'm going on a plane
I've never, ever been to Spain
I am going there
I have got a pink bikini
I can't wait to be there soon.

Demi Laurie (9)
Alexandra Parade Primary School, Glasgow

Good Holidays

I'm going on holiday
I'm going really soon
I'm going at the end of June
And I'm at the end of June
And I'm going on a plane to America
I am bursting to go to typhoon lagoon.

Graeme Hill (9)
Alexandra Parade Primary School, Glasgow

Sandy Beaches

I am going on my holidays
I don't know where
But I heard there is no snow there
I'm going to see the sun shining all day
The sandy beaches
And all the seashells upon them

The slight breeze at night
And the furry carpet in my room
Tickling my feet all night
There must be some palm trees
Waving all the time
The waves are cold
But the sun is bold

My mum said we are going to Tenerife
It's in Spain
We are going on a plane.

Lora Addison (8)
Alexandra Parade Primary School, Glasgow

The Pizza Holiday

I'm on my way to Italy
I'm going to have some fun
I'm going to munch some pizza
I'm going to have a run

I'm on my way to the sandy beach
I'm going to play some games
I'm going to have some fun
Now Lisa has got the game
So we've got the same.

Zoe Dorman (8)
Alexandra Parade Primary School, Glasgow

My Bikinis

I'm going on my holidays
I leave on the 5th June
I'm *bursting* with excitement
Because I'll be there soon

I'm going to eat some ice cream
And dive into the pool
I saw some lovely ladies
They thought I was really cool

I've got a pink bikini
I've got a green one too
In fact I've got a yellow one
But my favourite one is blue

I love all my bikinis
I wear them every day
I'm really, really happy
Because I'm here today!

Amy Brown (8)
Alexandra Parade Primary School, Glasgow

Holidays

I'm going on my holiday
I'm going to Turkey
I'm going to the hotel
I'm going to the pool
I'm going to the shower
I'm going to go on the roller coaster.

Cooper McCallum (8)
Alexandra Parade Primary School, Glasgow

Holiday

On holiday, some days
I went to the beach in my spare time,
I took my beach ball over there
And had some fun.

I had some fun,
I had a run.

I played over there and I went fishing,
Then we had some snacks
And went back to play.

I had some fun,
I had a run.

Finally we went back after we had played,
Then we all were talking about the beach
And how we had fun.

Shabaaz Ali (8)
Alexandra Parade Primary School, Glasgow

England

I'm going to England,
I'm going on a holiday.
I'm going to England,
I'm going for three weeks.
I'm going to my auntie's,
We'll go to the beach,
I'll put sand over my cousin,
I'll get an ice cream.

Lauren Daldry (8)
Alexandra Parade Primary School, Glasgow

Friends Forever

Friends forever,
Friends forever,
Friends wherever.

Friends are helpful,
Friends are cheerful.

Friends where?
Friends there,
Friends here.

Friends are helpful,
Friends are cheerful.

Friends are company,
Friends are funny,
Friends are playful.

Friends are helpful,
Friends are cheerful.

Devon Cameron (8)
Alexandra Parade Primary School, Glasgow

Two Weeks In Italy

I'm going away to Italy,
I'm going for two weeks,
I'm going to send you photos
And I hope there's no leaks.

I hope there's good doctors,
I hope there's good fruit there,
I like the canals,
I'd like not to run into a bear.

I can't wait to be there,
The pizza there is yum!
But even though I say that,
The spaghetti is even more scrummy.

James Reilly (9)
Alexandra Parade Primary School, Glasgow

Holidays

Holiday, holiday, totally fine
Hot, sandy, colourful, totally nice
The sun is shining all the time
You go through the beach in no time

The big blue sky
Is shining on my thigh
And it is burning so I will cry

Every year I go in the deep blue sea
One day I hurt my knee in the sea
Then my big sister went in the sea
She hurt her knee, then Santa came to see

The big blue sky
Is shining on my thigh
And it is burning
So I will cry.

Craig Brown (8)
Alexandra Parade Primary School, Glasgow

Friendship

Friends, friends everywhere
Friends, friends make you share

Friends, friends are kind
Friends, friends make you happy
Friends, friends care for you
Friends, friends share with you
Friends, friends make you laugh
Friends, friends tell you jokes

Friends, friends tell you spooky stories
Friends, friends play with you
Friends, friends keep you safe
Friends, friends should have fun.

Jamie Higgins (8)
Alexandra Parade Primary School, Glasgow

The Day We Went To The Beach

Sandy beach, sandy beach, people having fun,
People making sandcastles, people putting sun cream on,
People in the sea, some people are not
And some are having ice cream
Or some are just in the sun.

Fish in the sea,
People are wearing bikinis.

Seaweed everywhere, kids playing with shells,
Kids playing with buckets and spades
And some just in the arcade.
Mum and Dad looking for dolphins
Or just having a laugh.

Fish in the sea,
People are wearing bikinis.

Scott Hughes (8)
Alexandra Parade Primary School, Glasgow

Holidays

It is a sunny day on the beach
It is a sandy day on the beach

The sun is shining today
The sun is shining in the sky

The dolphins are going in and out the water
The fish are swimming in the sea

The sun is shining today
The sun is shining in the sky

I had fun today
I hope you did as well

The sun is shining today
The sun is shining in the sky.

Caitlin McNairney (8)
Alexandra Parade Primary School, Glasgow

Compass Christian Centre

C ool
O pinion, great
M eals, lovely
P laying in our spare time
A wesome
S cooby Doo
S unny weather

C limbing wall
H ere to stay for 4 nights
R isking getting to the top of the tree
I really enjoyed my stay
S ome rainy weather
T otally cool
I had a sore head
A greeing, not arguing
N ot too sleepy in the morning

C ompass TV live
E xcellent
N ow
T ime to leave
R aft building
E xciting.

Kerri Daniel (11)
Ardallie School, Peterhead

Celtic And Rangers

For Celtic and Rangers, Larsson and Moll
Are the players scoring goals
Celtic and Rangers are the best
Even though Martin O'Neil is taking a rest.

Craig Grubb (8)
Ardallie School, Peterhead

The Disgusting Cake

First of all you take a bowl
Then put in a hairy mole
Take some milk and then a quilt
Take a dog and then a frog
Add them all to the bowl
Then you'll get your lovely cake sold
But we're not finished yet
There's still some ingredients to get
There's hogs, frogs, crocodiles' jaws
Muddy footballs and cats' beautiful claws
Add some butter and then some flowers
Your mixture is ready, now you just have to heat it
Now it's ready and really, really hot
Let me taste my beautiful cake, *oh yuck!*

Zaenab Mahmood (9)
Ardallie School, Peterhead

My Path

I have a path
Leading to a bath
In the bath
There was a calf

Behind the bath
Was another path
Leading to a lake

In the lake
There was a steak
I ate the steak
And drank the lake

I became fat
And that was that.

Bruce Grubb (11)
Ardallie School, Peterhead

Red Rage!

I am a volcano on the verge of eruption
I am a bull ready to charge
There's a red devil burning inside me
Waiting to break free
Fire in my eyes
Veins throbbing
Neck burning
Fists clenched
The storm strikes
I jump up
Thump down
Palms banging
Feet stomping
I am mad with
Rage . . .
Red rage!

Megan McKenzie (11)
Balmullo Primary School, St Andrews

Nothing Left

My red face oozes with sweat!
I feel fire in my mouth like a dragon.
My feet stamp on the ground,
I squeeze my hands till they are numb.
I jump on the beds,
I bang on the walls,
I rip up paper,
I pour out all the juice,
I shout with rage,
Until
I've nothing left!

Linzi Brunton (11)
Balmullo Primary School, St Andrews

Out Of Control

My face red as fire
My neck hot and sweaty

I stamp my feet
Like a spoilt brat

I'm a bull ready
To charge

The devil inside me
Urging to get out

I simmer until
I explode!

The table
Lies broken!

Ross Christie (12)
Balmullo Primary School, St Andrews

Red Rage

My red-hot face boils like hot lava
My fists clench and sweat like a dragon crushing a mouse
A rhino on a rampage
I stamp on anyone in my path

Everlasting fire burns
Through my flesh
Speeding cars rush through my soul crashing
Against brick walls
Steaming like a kettle
I hiss and scream.

David Drew (10)
Balmullo Primary School, St Andrews

Bored

My eyes bore into the back of the boy's head
I twiddle with my thumbs
I shuffle about in my seat until my bottom is sore
Slowly I run my fingers through my hair
And then stare into space

I watch the people running about outside
I yawn, stretch
And put my head on the desk
I swing on my chair
And then study a spider slowly spinning a web

'Fraser!' my teacher shouts
'Pay attention!'

Fraser Simpson (12)
Balmullo Primary School, St Andrews

What Is The Moon?

The moon is a star
In the middle of space

It is a cold spotlight
Staring from a black ceiling

It is a golden light
At the end of a dark tunnel

It is a shining light
That lights up the night

It is a light in
The darkness of night.

Matthew McGuire (12)
Balmullo Primary School, St Andrews

Eruption

I erupt like Mt Vesuvius
Making the ground tremble as I stamp my feet in anger
I begin to build a rage
My neck is as hot as boiling water
I clench my fists until they go white
As the burning rage inside me breaks free
And I lose self-control
I begin to destroy the table that lies in front of me
I explode like a bomb
Sweat pours down, past the
Inferno that fills my eyes
I roar, my throat boiling
Like a dragon ready to breathe fire
My rage is never-ending, as I feel another

Eruption!

Dominic Stewart (12)
Balmullo Primary School, St Andrews

The Lonely Bat

(Based on 'I Wandered Lonely As A Cloud' by William Wordsworth)

I wandered lonely as a bat
That I thought I was a pussy cat
When suddenly I saw a shark
The colour of a kangaroo
When next I saw a quacking duck
With spots upon his bill
I just dropped from my perch and hit my head
And knew I was most definitely dead.

Steven Harris (11)
Balmullo Primary School, St Andrews

Sadness

I feel cold and lifeless
Everything around me seems grey
All my limbs go limp
My eyes turn icy-blue

My dry eyes want to cry
But there's nothing
Every drop of energy gone down the drain
I want to kick and scream
But all my nerves feel pain

My head feels light
Yet I can't stop it from hanging
My legs give way
I fall to the ground and melt into a puddle.

Robbie Docherty (11)
Balmullo Primary School, St Andrews

What Is The Moon?

The moon is as cold as ice
Like a light in the sky

It is a white ball
Playing on a black pitch

A 50p coin
Falling from a black purse

A white plate
Spinning on invisible wire

A white snowball
Flying through the night.

Jai Frape (11)
Balmullo Primary School, St Andrews

The Dolphins' Plea

I have a mind full of wishes
I want a nice ocean to swim in all day long
I don't want fishing nets
Which fill me with fear
I want to swim around a pollution free sea
Jumping in and out of blue water
I would like a supply of shrimps
To eat all day long

I am a smooth piece of velvet
Flying underwater
People say I bite but I don't
I am a loving creature
My skin shimmers in the calm, clear sea
Darts are slow compared to me
But all I want is to love and be loved
So next time you're dumping oil in the sea
Think of my skin, think of its smoothness
Think about my friendship.

Craig Spence (11)
Balmullo Primary School, St Andrews

The Pink Lipgloss

So much depends
Upon

The pink lip
Gloss

Lying on the
Unit

Beside the black
Mascara.

Nicole Hunter (11)
Balmullo Primary School, St Andrews

Away From My Bedroom Cage

I walk down the bright green football pitch,
On my way to boarding school, happy
To be away from my bedroom cage,
Excited to think I won't have to go there till summer.

My feet bounce along the school corridor,
Echoing like thunder in a cave,
My voice is loud and happy as I
Joke and laugh with my friends.

I am quickest to react on sports day,
Scoring goals and tries.
It is so amazing to have so much freedom,
So happy, so relieved to be away from home.

Matthew Childs (12)
Balmullo Primary School, St Andrews

Fluffy Clouds

(Based on 'I Wandered Lonely As A Cloud' by William Wordsworth)

I wandered lonely as a car
That drives along the hardened tar
When suddenly I saw a herd of cows
The colour of fluffy clouds
When next I saw a splattered cat
Walking along like an acrobat
I swerved left and shouted 'Beep!'
And knew I'd hit a sheep.

Lee Thomson (11)
Balmullo Primary School, St Andrews

Heavy-Hearted

I sit in a dark, shadowy corner,
Cold, lonely, shedding floods of tears,
In a world of my own,
All black like the cloudy night sky,
I scream at the top of my lungs,
But nothing comes out,
I wish the ground would swallow me up,
Thoughts and words remain unsaid,
I know it's my fault!

Nicole Graham (11)
Balmullo Primary School, St Andrews

My Pet

My pet doesn't have a wing
My pet's got no fur
My pet doesn't fly or walk
My pet doesn't talk
My pet isn't furry but it's one you won't mistake
For my pet is a swishy, wishy,
Slippy, dippy, intelligent,
Life-saving dolphin.

Sophie Booth (9)
Bankhead Primary School, Rutherglen

Here Lies The Body Of . . .

Here lies the body of a mouse by the clock
He paid the bill and went tick-tock!

Here lies the body of the man on the moon
He did not feel well, so he ate a spoon!

Kirsty Allison (9)
Bankhead Primary School, Rutherglen

Here Lies The Body

Here lies the body
Of a mouse by a clock
Who wanted to talk?
When the clock went tick-tock

Here lies the body
Of Old King Cole
Who broke his toe
On a piece of coal.

Bianca Muir (10)
Bankhead Primary School, Rutherglen

My Pet

My pet has no tail
My pet is not a whale
My pet's not got fur
My pet doesn't purr
My pet doesn't bark or sing
She's one you won't forget
For my pet is an intelligent, life-saving dolphin.

Angela Vincent (9)
Bankhead Primary School, Rutherglen

Sunflowers

Sunflowers growing
Under the sky
Mercy, mercy for fresh air
More sun every day
Everyone having fun
Rising sun is setting.

Chloe Sanders (9)
Bankhead Primary School, Rutherglen

Christmas Acrostic

C andy canes around the Christmas tree
H appy families everywhere you can see
R eindeers flying by the window sill
I cing on the cake as sweet as candy cane
S tockings on the chimney wall
T rees so very, very tall
M istletoe where everyone is kissed
A ngels who made up the Christmas list
S anta Claus who makes every kid happy.

Claire Moore (10)
Bankhead Primary School, Rutherglen

My Family

M y family are as funny as can be
Y ou really want to know why? Well come and see

F un and loving we may be, but you really don't want to run into me
A m mad as a hatter, silly as can be
M y dad has big blue eyes and wobbly knees
I f you want to know how my mum looks, she looks really mad
L oving we may be, but you should taste my granny's cooking -
really, really bad!
Y ou may think I am mad, but I don't care! See you soon!

Kim Dornan (9)
Bankhead Primary School, Rutherglen

The Man In The Moon

(Inspired by 'The Man in the Moon')

Here lies the body of the man in the moon
Fell off the moon and landed in a spoon.

Josh Mackay (10)
Bankhead Primary School, Rutherglen

Birthday Acrostic

B oys and girls get lots of presents on their birthday.
I nside boxes all shapes and sizes are lots of surprises.
R ising early in the morning, can't wait to get downstairs.
T he candles melt as they get lit.
H ip hip hooray is being sung everywhere.
D ad and Mum got me the best present ever.
A mazing atmosphere at my party.
Y es, my birthday is today.
S uper presents that I got on my birthday I play with all the time.

Jenna Reid (9)
Bankhead Primary School, Rutherglen

Football Is My Favourite Sport

F ootball is my favourite sport
O n the park you must not swear
O n the park you must be fair
T ime to score for your team
B eyond the tunnel there's a match
A ll the fans in celebration
L istening to others shout and sing
L ooking at your favourite players lifting the cup.

Greg Cowan (9)
Bankhead Primary School, Rutherglen

Here Lies The Bodies Of Jack And Jill
(Inspired by 'Jack and Jill' and 'The Man in the Moon')

Here lies the bodies of Jack and Jill
They fell down a hill and they were very ill

Here lies the body of the man on the moon
He soon got hit with a giant spoon.

Graeme Dickie (10)
Bankhead Primary School, Rutherglen

Football

F ootball is my sport
O n the pitch you must not swear
O ut playing in my new kit
T eam mates are passing to me
B ut I get a pass and it is a goal
A player gets hurt
L et me get a penalty
L et me get another goal and the fans will be saying, 'What a goal!'

Barry Lawrie (9)
Bankhead Primary School, Rutherglen

Winter Acrostic

W inter is here
I cy day
N ippy wind
T ime passing on
E verybody is cold
R esting all day.

Adelle Brown (9)
Bankhead Primary School, Rutherglen

Temper

T emper is
E vil, it
M akes nice
P eople fall out with
E veryone they love and
R obs them of their dignity.

Lauren McPherson (10)
Bankhead Primary School, Rutherglen

Seasons Acrostic

S ummer's nearly here
P ink blossom on trees
R unning freely
I nhaling the fresh air
N ew green leaves
G reat world outdoors

S unlight sparkling
U nbelievable temperatures
M assive yachts
M arvellous meadows
E normous elms
R esting in the sea

A nimals hibernating
U nderneath conifers
T ime passing by
U mbrellas soaking wet
M any misty mornings
N ippy days

W ind wailing
I cy rivers
N ever-ending snow
T ime travelling slowly
E verything is white
R eally good snowmen.

Martin Tracey (10)
Bankhead Primary School, Rutherglen

The Three Blind Mice

(Inspired by 'Three Blind Mice')

Here lies the body of
Three blind mice
Banged into a wall
And did not look nice.

William MacPherson (10)
Bankhead Primary School, Rutherglen

Vandalism

V ulgar words written on walls
A lcoholic drinks are dropped on roads and pavements
N on-stop graffiti on walls, doors and windows
D amaged cars and houses
A lleys have been spray painted
L itter has been dumped on the ground
I t is illegal to vandalise other people's property
S omeone has to make it stop
M any people vandalise, stop the habit now!

Luke Pye (10)
Bankhead Primary School, Rutherglen

The Football Acrostic

F ootball is my favourite sport
O n the field you must not swear
O n the field you have to be fair
T ime to play when you're ready
B eyond the tunnel there are your heroes
A bove the field there are lots of fans
L ooking at the crowd
L ifting the trophy.

David Stephen (9)
Bankhead Primary School, Rutherglen

Emotion Poem

Evil is red as my blood
Like the taste of red-hot chilli
And the smell of fire that's just been put out
Evil looks like a devil
And sounds like a hideous laugh
Evil feels like razor-sharp spikes.

Dylan McDermott (9)
Bankhead Primary School, Rutherglen

A Poem About Feelings

I'm as happy as a dog with its big juicy bone.
I'm as happy as a cat in a bar of big mice.
I'm as lonely as a cat in an abandoned hospital.
I'm as sad as an elephant without my tusks.
I'm as unhappy as a shark that's lost its sharp teeth.
I'm as happy as a monkey swinging from the trees.
I'm as sad as a cat in an abandoned school.
I'm as lonely as a zebra without its long black stripes.

Jordan McNaught (9)
Bankhead Primary School, Rutherglen

Battle Of Bannockburn

Claymores crashing and lots of killing.
Swords stabbing and slashing.
People's heads being sliced off.
I am terrified but now I am brave.
My heart is bouncing up and down.
All I can hear is horses neighing lollily.
I feel confident victory is near.

Kerry McNeice (9)
Bankhead Primary School, Rutherglen

Emotion Poem

Evil is as black as rain-filled clouds
Tastes like rotten old eggs in your mouth
It smells like dirty socks hanging up in the house
Looks like dark vampire's teeth full of blood
Sounds like a creaky old door squeaking in a spooky old house
It feels like yucky, gooey mud oozing all over your body.

Howe Yee Shing (10)
Bankhead Primary School, Rutherglen

Save The . . .

Save the whale
Save the whale
Cos it's got a great big tail

Save the tiger
Save the tiger
Because it doesn't eat the giant panda

Save the monkey
Save the monkey
Cos it's furry and is funky

Save the world
Save the world
Let's stop using solid fuel.

Lauren McArthur (11)
Bankhead Primary School, Rutherglen

Despair

Despair is pale like a face.
Like the taste of vomit in your mouth
And the smell of out-of-date cheese.
Despair looks like nothing
And sounds like a bird.
Despair feels cold like ice.

Nicola Mitchell (8)
Bankhead Primary School, Rutherglen

Jack And Jill

(Inspired by 'Jack and Jill')

Here lies the bodies
Of Jack and Jill
They fetched a pail of water
And fell down a well.

Gavin Irvine (10)
Bankhead Primary School, Rutherglen

My Cat

I have a cat
She isn't fat
She is very stripy

Her name is Molly
She is very jolly
And likes to play

Her favourite food is fish
She eats it from a dish
And then she sleeps on my bed.

Megan Young (10)
Bankhead Primary School, Rutherglen

Here Lies The Body

(Inspired by 'Old King Cole')

Here lies the body
Of Old King Cole
He was very old
And he died with the cold

Here lies the body
Of the man in the moon
He got hit with a giant spoon.

Adam Stewart (9)
Bankhead Primary School, Rutherglen

Where Did They Go?

(Based on 'Jack and Jill')

Here lies the body of Jack and Jill
Hit by a horse, fell down the hill.

Jay Prentice (9)
Bankhead Primary School, Rutherglen

Battle Of Independence: Bannockburn

What do you see?
Horses covered in blood
Spears and claymores clashing
Clattering and crashing
Onto the ground

What do you feel?
Terror
I could die
My heart bouncing like a trampoline

What do you hear?
Footsteps getting closer and closer
Men shouting
'Freedom!'
Victory is ours.

Craig Dallas (10)
Bankhead Primary School, Rutherglen

Big Brothers

Some are fab, some are tall,
My brother drives me up the wall.
Some are crazy, some are wee,
But all mine does is watch TV.

When he plays golf, he's really cool,
He sometimes beats my dad at pool.
His club music is quite funky,
Although who knows, he could turn punky.

Some are kind, some are weedy,
Mine used to fancy Cheryl Tweedy.
After this, it's plain to see,
My fave *Big Brother* is on TV.

Melissa Crabb (10)
Bankhead Primary School, Rutherglen

A Poem About Feelings

I am as happy as a giraffe with its tall long neck
Eating at the leaves

I am as happy as a dog in its kennel
Chewing at his bone

I am as lonely as a monkey swinging
From tree to tree by myself

I'm as sad as a zebra without its
Black and white stripes

I'm as happy as a horse
Galloping round itself

I'm as happy as an elephant
With my long trunk waving in the air

I'm as sad as a kitten
Who's lost its mum

I'm as lonely as a dolphin
With no fish swimming by.

Ciara Tollan (9)
Bankhead Primary School, Rutherglen

Emotion Poem

Fear is black like paint
Smudging on a bit of paper
Like the taste of saliva
Going around your mouth
And the smell of rotten egg
Sizzling in a pan
Fear looks as black
As a bridge at night
And sounds like a crocodile
Snapping at someone
Fear feels like bees buzzing around me.

Susanne Shaw (9)
Bankhead Primary School, Rutherglen

A Poem About Feelings

I'm as happy as a cat with a barn full of mice.
I'm as happy as a great white shark in a beach full of people.
I'm as lonely as a mouse in a shut-down factory.
I'm as sad as a bird with nothing to eat.
I'm as unhappy as a shark that's lost his razor-sharp teeth.
I'm as happy as an eagle that's just hatched a new baby.
I'm as sad as an eagle that's just lost its new baby.
I'm as lonely as a cat in an abandoned hospital.

Jodie Brannan (8)
Bankhead Primary School, Rutherglen

A Poem About Feelings

I'm as happy as a zebra with black and white stripes.
I'm as happy as a cat in a barn with a lot of mice.
I'm as lonely as a dog in a factory with no one to look after him.
I'm as sad as a horse without its friend.
I'm as unhappy as a lion that's lost its tail.
I'm as happy as a cat with a home to live in.
I'm as sad as a dog that has no owner.
I'm as lonely as a lion that's lost its baby.

Jordan Wallace (8)
Bankhead Primary School, Rutherglen

A Poem About Feelings

I'm as happy as a dog with a toy, nice and blue.
I'm as happy as a dolphin in a big blue sea.
I'm as lonely as a cat with no friends in the dark.
I'm as sad as a fish in a big net.
I'm as unhappy as an ant that's lost its mum in the dark night.
I'm as happy as a crocodile eating a fish in the water.
I'm as lonely as a monkey that's lost in the green dark jungle.

Joshua Hurley (8)
Bankhead Primary School, Rutherglen

A Poem About Feelings

I'm as happy as a monkey with a jungle full of bananas.
I'm as happy as a snake in a barn full of rats.
I'm as lonely as a cat in a shut-down factory.
I'm as sad as a shark that's lost its teeth.
I'm unhappy as a lion that's lost its baby.
I'm as happy as a frog in a pond full of stones.
I'm as sad as a tiger that's lost its stripes.
I'm as lonely as a bird in a cage.

Robert Hamilton (8)
Bankhead Primary School, Rutherglen

A Poem About Feelings

I'm as happy as a monkey with a banana in its hand
I'm as happy as a giraffe in a lovely zoo
I'm as lonely as a shark in a deep blue sea
I'm as sad as a cheetah without its agility to run
I'm as unhappy as a foal that's lost its mum
I'm as happy as a monkey swinging in the trees
I'm as sad as a baby zebra tripping over its legs
I'm as lonely as a grasshopper jumping on the grass.

Jordan McPhee (8)
Bankhead Primary School, Rutherglen

A Poem Of Feelings

I'm as happy as a dog with a bone in its mouth
I'm as happy as a tortoise in its shell sleeping
I'm as lonely as a squirrel with no nuts to eat on a tree
I'm as sad as a zebra without its black and white stripes
I'm as unhappy as a cat that's lost its mum
I'm as happy as a horse in a stable eating hay
I'm as sad as a tiger that's lost its claws
I'm as lonely as a dolphin with no fish to swim with.

Lisa McPherson (8)
Bankhead Primary School, Rutherglen

The Haunted House

At the haunted house,
Where no one dared to go,
There were old scary trees,
With branches big and heavy,
That many people saw as they passed in horror!
Inside the house were old paintings
That hung on the wall,
Of old ancient Egyptians,
There was candlelight
That lit up the long, dark corridors,
There were big spooky shadows,
Creeping along each wall,
It was cold as the wind swept past,
Whispering cries for help,
All inside the haunted house!

Megan Stewart (10)
Bankhead Primary School, Rutherglen

A Contrast Poem

Alone
When you are alone, you feel sad and miserable.
The room echoes with emptiness.
Light the fire but there's only a slight spark.
Lie on the bed but it feels empty and cold.
Decorate the Christmas tree with no friends to help.

Together
When you're together with family and friends, you feel happy.
The room filled with cheers and laughter.
Light the fire and it's a welcoming blaze.
Lie on the bed and it feels warm and cosy.
Decorate the Christmas tree with family and friends.

Georgina Ely (10)
Bankhead Primary School, Rutherglen

My Birthday

On the night before my birthday,
Which I call my birthday eve,
I dream about all my presents
And never want the excitement to leave.

I wake up and realise,
That finally the day has come,
My mum begins to get everything ready,
While she happily starts to hum.

I tear open all of my presents,
Seeing stuff I dreamed to get,
I had a party with all my friends,
Which was at the countryside fête.

It gets a little later,
So it's time for my birthday tea,
I finish my food, it's time for the cake,
Everybody starts to sing 'Happy Birthday' to me.

The day is nearing the end,
It's the end of the 5th of May,
What a wonderful time I've had,
Today on my birthday.

Lauren McGugan (11)
Bankhead Primary School, Rutherglen

Love

Love is red like strawberries
It sounds like people dancing to romantic music
It tastes like strawberries in your mouth
It looks like two people having a romantic evening
It feels like two people kissing
It reminds me of Romeo and Juliet.

Ashleigh Curran (8)
Bankhead Primary School, Rutherglen

Blue

Blue is the colour I like
Blue is the colour of my bike
I like blue and pink
Pink makes the boys wink
Blue is a boys colour and also a drink
I love pink, it's the best
And it is also the colour of some ink
Blue is the colour of my soap next to my sink
Blue is the colour of my skates
When I go on the ice rink
And there is no such thing as a blue link.

Kirsty Howard (10)
Bankhead Primary School, Rutherglen

The Life

Greasy fatty foods make smelly fatty kids,
McDonald's and fast food, those are bad for you.
Don't eat burgers, too much fat,
Exercise is good for you.
So don't just be a couch potato,
Get out and about,
Down to the gym
To burn off those calories.

Gregor Campbell (11)
Banton Primary School, Glasgow

A Day At The Zoo

Monkey, monkey, sitting in a tree
Monkey, monkey, looking down at me
Monkey, monkey, what do you see?
'A cheeky little monkey looking back at me.'

Emma Stewart (11)
Banton Primary School, Glasgow

Why Is It?

Why is it that the sky is blue?
Why is it that the grass is green?
Why is it that the yellow sun is shining on me?
Why is it that the horizon is so orange and pink?
Why is it that the seas and oceans are turquoise green?
Why is it that when someone in my family say
That they love me, I get a warm feeling inside?
Why is it when I see my friends, they brighten up my day?
Why is it when night falls I have my dreams till dawn?

Rebecca MacAngus (11)
Banton Primary School, Glasgow

Eat Healthily

Healthy food is good for you.
Brushing your teeth and exercising too.
Sleeping and eating fruit.
Drinking apple juice.
Chips and chocolate, kids like to eat,
Don't be lazy,
Eat healthily!

Lucy Thomson (10)
Banton Primary School, Glasgow

Food

H am is my sister's favourite
E ggs are my dad's
A pples are my mum's favourite
L ettuce is my gran's
T omatoes are my favourite but
H otdogs are my uncle Robert's
Y oghurts are my auntie Ann's.

Megan Adam (11)
Banton Primary School, Glasgow

Healthy Eating

E ating healthy won't leave you fat.
A lways eat healthy wherever you're at.
T ake a piece of fruit every day.

H ealthy eating is the good way.
E xercise is great for you.
A nytime you start is good too.
L ive a healthy lifestyle.
T hen you might be able to run a mile.
H ave some fruit every day.
Y ou'll notice the difference in lots of ways.

George Douglas (11)
Banton Primary School, Glasgow

Health

H ealth is important
E at fruit and you will feel brand new
A lways remember to brush your teeth
L earn to wash hands often
T ake care of your body
H ave a happy, healthy life.

Nicole Cameron (10)
Banton Primary School, Glasgow

Health

H ave five fruit and veg every day.
E xercise to keep you fit.
A pples and apricots for lunch.
L aughing and playing, it's so much fun.
T each other children what you know.
H appily running around the pitch.

Bonnie Cameron (11)
Banton Primary School, Glasgow

Exercise

E very day do one hour of exercise.

eX ercise is fun.

E nergy levels high.

R aspberries are good for you.

C hips are very bad.

I ce cream can be tasty.

S atsumas juicy.

E nough energy to do that work-out.

Michael McMillan (11)
Banton Primary School, Glasgow

Healthy

H ealthy food is good for you

E xercise every day

A n apple a day keeps the doctor away

L ive healthily

T ake time to sleep

H appy lives, a healthy life

Y ou don't want to be like a hippo.

Gemma Gilmour (11)
Banton Primary School, Glasgow

Banton

B ecause Banton is small, it is

A very nice place

N o violence

T eachers in Banton Primary are cool

O ne shop, a dam and a community hall

N o village like it.

John Paterson (10)
Banton Primary School, Glasgow

Healthy Living!

H ealthy living!
E xercise each day,
A pples help you in every way.
L ie in when you have the chance,
T angerines make me want to dance.
H ealthy foods are
Y ummy, so put them in your *tummy!*

Rachel Wilson (10)
Banton Primary School, Glasgow

Bundle Of Joy
(For a newborn baby I know)

It's a girl
And she's beautiful
She's a little
Bundle of joy

Soon we'll have
To buy
Her a soft
Cuddly toy

With her little
Cute face
And her little
Round hat
She'll look so happy
And that's that!

Eve Lucas (11)
Burnside Primary School, Rutherglen

Fear

Fear is dark blue like a night shadow.
It sounds like a nasty wolf when it's a full moon.
It tastes like a rotten and sour melon.
It smells like the dark and cold winds of the night.
It feels like a terribly hot burn in your head.

Josh Weir (10)
Craigielea Primary School, Paisley

Blue

Blue is the colour
Of our superb uniform.

Blue is the colour
Of our deep, dark sky at night.

Blue is the colour
Of the bright clear sea.

Blue is the colour
Of the superlative crystals.

Neil Carter (10)
Craigielea Primary School, Paisley

Happiness

Happiness is yellow like a beautiful buttercup.
It sounds like lovely calming music.
It tastes like lovely ice cream and melon.
It smells like the breezy air and lovely woods.
It feels like a warm lovely pillow.

Stewart Bruce (10)
Craigielea Primary School, Paisley

Blue

Blue is the colour
of my brand new sweatshirt.

Blue is the colour
of my school marker.

Blue is the colour
of my pencil case.

Blue is the colour
of my old bobble.

Paige Gilchrist (9)
Craigielea Primary School, Paisley

Blue

Blue is the colour
of our lovely bright school uniform.

Blue is the colour
of an exciting holiday with colourful water.

Blue is the colour
of a summer sky with a little breeze.

Blue is the colour
of a shiny, new ball.

Callum Colvin (10)
Craigielea Primary School, Paisley

Happiness

Happiness is yellow like the nice sunrise.
It sounds like the birds chirping in the branches.
It tastes like a delicious bar of chocolate.
It smells like the beautiful flowers in the wind.
It feels like a beautiful cuddly soft toy.

Robert Larkin (9)
Craigielea Primary School, Paisley

Blue

Blue is the colour
Of our dark and heavy jumper.

Blue is the colour
Of our soft tie.

Blue is the colour
Of the sunny sky.

Blue is the colour
Of the primary dictionary.

Demi Stewart (9)
Craigielea Primary School, Paisley

Blue

Blue is the colour
Of the bright coloured pencil.

Blue is the colour
Of the deep dark sea.

Blue is the colour
Of my ice-cold freezer.

Blue is the colour
Of the money-making diamonds.

Katie Davidson (9)
Craigielea Primary School, Paisley

Sadness

Sadness is blue like a lazy, fat whale.
It sounds like an animal in pain.
It tastes like a horrible blue piranha.
It smells like a dead fish coming out of the water.

Jay Stewart (10)
Craigielea Primary School, Paisley

Blue

Blue is the colour of some butterflies
flying around in the sky.

Blue is the colour of my big lovely cool room.

Blue is the colour of me when I am very excited.

Blue is the colour of my nice clean lost sweater.

Andrew Carter (10)
Craigielea Primary School, Paisley

Happiness

Happiness is yellow like the beautiful sunny sky.
It sounds like the water flowing.
It tastes like a nice cold ice cream.
It smells like a delicious chocolate cake.
It feels like the nice soft sand.

Demi Foulds (10)
Craigielea Primary School, Paisley

Sadness

Sadness is blue, like a baby when it wants its bottle.
It sounds like rain when it's battering off your face.
It tastes like a blueberry ice-pole.
It smells like chlorine in the swimming pool.
It feels like snow when it's gently falling on the ground.

Alison Burgess (10)
Craigielea Primary School, Paisley

Unhappiness

Unhappiness is blue like a light bright sky.
It sounds like a falling yellow star.
It tastes like an over-cooked cake.
It smells like a salty cup of tea.
It feels like a hard piece of wood.

Tammi Cameron (10)
Craigielea Primary School, Paisley

Sadness

Sadness is violet like dead bluebells.
It sounds like snow falling on a dark winter's night.
It tastes like a burnt bit of toast stuck in your throat.
It smells like a horrible piece of rubbish from the bin.
It feels like coldness creeping in the window.

Lauren Kidd (10)
Craigielea Primary School, Paisley

Blue

Blue is the colour of the bright shiny sea.
Blue is the colour of some fish swimming in the sea.
Blue is the colour of the bluebells swaying in the wind.
Blue is the colour of the great whale spraying water from
                                    the top of its head.

Cameron Thomson (10)
Craigielea Primary School, Paisley

Blue

Blue is the colour of our bright jumper.
Blue is the colour of my short tie.
Blue is the colour of the world's light sky.
Blue is the colour of our dark dictionaries.

Jordan Gemmell (9)
Craigielea Primary School, Paisley

Crazy

Crazy is black like the thunderous sky.
It sounds like an earthquake shaking the ground.
It tastes like a red hot chilli.
It smells like a boiling hot lava monster.
It feels like a boiling head that is about to stop.

Rebecca Bools (9)
Craigielea Primary School, Paisley

The Giraffe

I am a giraffe strolling across the open plains of Africa,
I can see big tall trees scattered everywhere.
Lions, cheetahs and other big cats hunting for a meal.
Other animals fighting the hippos, looking for a mate.

Patches of lush green grass,
Hunters hiding in the bushes,
What will I do if he sees me?

I can hear lions roaring from miles away
And leopards prowling through the grass,
Will I get caught . . . or will I get away?

Monkeys making an awful noise,
Are they having a party?
Hippos fighting in the water over their homes.

I feel alone and unprotected without my family,
Angry about the hunter catching animals for no reason,
Scared in case the hunter gets me.

Chloe Vass (10)
Duncan Forbes Primary School, Inverness

Under The Sea

Come under the sea and play with me,
There's lots of things for you to see,
My friends and family,
Exotic plants for you and me,
Every fish to light up your face with glee.

Come under the sea and play with me,
There's lots of things you can hear,
Dolphins calling in your ear.
Anchors dropping to the rear,
Fishes' tails coming near.

Come under the sea and play with me,
There's lots of things for you to feel,
Frightened of sharks and what they might steal,
Amazed at the fishes and their meal,
Nerves at everything that's real.

Come under the sea and play with me,
There's lots of things for you to do,
Laugh and giggle like you,
Explore the ocean too,
There's so many things you can do.

Come under the sea and play with me,
There's lots of things you can find,
Starfish hiding from behind,
A nice little family that look so kind,
Come under the sea and play with me.

Eilidh Campbell (11)
Duncan Forbes Primary School, Inverness

The Circus

Jolly music buzzing in my ears,
Rustling of sweet packets and the chewing of candyfloss,
Clapping after my wonderful juggling trick,
Laughter from the audience all around me.

I feel happy and excited, but nervous at the same time,
I look all round me, left, right
And I begin to feel more and more anxious,
Then people laugh at me
So I start to feel good about myself.

I can see the silvery seals jumping through a ring of fire,
Lions roaring in their huge metal cage,
All the other clowns are juggling their brightly coloured balls,
I can see the enormous audience with adults,
Children and babies watching me.

Now my show is nearly over, only thirty minutes left,
My last trick is juggling fire sticks
And I don't know if I can do it,
Here we go very slowly, take a big breath and . . .
I made it, now I have done the circus show!

Rebecca Waugh (11)
Duncan Forbes Primary School, Inverness

War Poem

It's wartime and children are scared
The dark skies light up with bombs and flares
The sirens go off and we all run like rabbits and hares

London has been bombed yet again
Will we ever get out of this dingy old den?
The humdrum of planes overhead
How many this time will be dead?

Brave men fight for their lives
Many have left their children and their wives
Will they ever return again? No one knows
God will be with them wherever they go

The sirens have stopped
The town's ablaze
Smoke and ashes fill the skies
The distress is shown in everyone's eyes

Soon this will be over and all will be well
We will try to rebuild our lives and our country
The skies will be clear again, the sun will always be there
This will be a great story to tell.

Ellen McKenzie (11)
Duncan Forbes Primary School, Inverness

Sea Life

Come deep down under the sea,
With lots of other fish just like me,
Multicoloured creatures
And green seaweed,
Come deep down under the sea.

Come deep down under the sea,
Hear the splashing of the dolphins,
Come with me!
Hear the mermaids singing beautifully,
Come deep down under the sea.

Come deep down under the sea,
Be happy just like me.
We are messing about and we're having fun,
Now the sharks are coming . . .
We'd better *run!*

Come deep down under the sea,
I am kind of frightened
Because they are right behind me!
Snapping their jaws
And swimming with glee,
Thinking they are going to catch me,
Come deep down under the sea.

Come deep down under the sea,
The sharks have gone,
Now we're jumping with glee.
I hope you come back another time,
Come deep down under the sea.

Alyssa Cook (11)
Duncan Forbes Primary School, Inverness

Hunting

Here I am standing silently in the forest,
Waiting for my prey to emerge from the bushes.
My fox cub is tormenting the ducks in the pond
And the birds are flapping their wings so violently
It sounds like a big bass drum.

Rabbits are hopping everywhere,
They shall be my prey.
Suddenly I see an orange figure,
It's my cub pouncing on the rabbit,
Oh no, he has scared them away.

My stomach is rumbling,
My cub is whimpering for he has not eaten since yesterday,
There is the faint barking of a dog,
The hunter is loading his gun,
The barn owl is awake and frantically tu-whit tu-whooing.

The woodpecker is thumping the birch tree for a special caterpillar,
The branches are rustling making me nervous
As I move through the forest,
The birds are tweeting,
They seem happy and content
And the ducks are quacking playfully at one another.

I am scared, the animals are fleeing everywhere,
I feel anxious because I hear the panting of a huge dog.
I can feel only mortal danger,
I am in dreadful pain,
The hunter has aimed a blow from his gun at me,
I feel my soul has been taken away,
The hunter has claimed another skin.

Hayley Smyth (10)
Duncan Forbes Primary School, Inverness

The Battle Of Stirling

As my soldiers stand on the steep bay of Stirling
The rain hurling on brave Scots' brows
I feel proud of my army of powerful Scots
Many's the battle that they have fought

I see all around me, bloodthirsty men
My Scots ready to kill the English again
I hear shields shattering
Swords clashing and angry cries

I feel the cold sting of a blade tear my flesh
Though I am in pain
I'll carry on fighting for my country
Time and time again

A man is running at me
So I stick my sword in his gut
He falls to the ground
I hear arrows flying through the air

I get a steady aim
And release my arrow
I kill my target
I'm proud to be a clan chief.

Calum Green (10)
Duncan Forbes Primary School, Inverness

Elephants

I am an elephant strolling through the jungle.
I can see all the lush green trees,
Petals shining in the sun,
Water coming from the river
And monkeys hanging from the trees.

I can hear the lions roaring,
The hunters stamping through the leaves,
The rustling through the trees,
Through the quiet wind and breeze.

I am feeling scared and all on my own,
I wish I had just somebody here,
So I won't be alone.

The hunters have found me, what will I do?
They have surrounded me all at once,
Nowhere to go, nowhere to run,
There goes the noise of that awful big gun.

The silly fools have missed again,
I think I'll make a run for it.
I'll go for a short-cut I know the best,
Through the jungle I'll just have a rest.

Chelsea Bolt (10)
Duncan Forbes Primary School, Inverness

Going To School

It's half past eight, I'm nearly late,
I dash out the door as quick as an ape.
I run as fast as I can to Eilidh's door,
I hope, I hope she's ready in time,
I ring the doorbell, the door opens.
My heart is pounding like a big bass drum,
The school gate's in sight, let's run! run! run!
Eilidh huffs and puffs as we head for the gate,
I've promised myself an early night tonight
And we won't be late.
We have arrived in school just in time,
Uniform is still spick and span,
Mum would be proud if she would see how tidy I am.
I'm on my way home, happy as a happy hippo,
Tomorrow is another day,
I hope I am never late, ever again.

Charis Crawford-Mair (11)
Duncan Forbes Primary School, Inverness

Happiness

Happiness is a river skipping over pebble stones,
as clear as day.

Happiness is like the fluff of a cotton plant dancing,
slowly floating off their stems into the air.

Happiness is a tree blooming in the spring,
leaves as vivid as a summer's day.

Happiness is the sound of happy children playing in the sun,
jumping, skipping, running, having lots of fun!

Emma Haines (10)
Fort William RC Primary School, Fort William

Sadness

Sadness is a slow river of emotions,
Flowing down the mountain.

Sadness strikes when it rains black tears,
From the dark, damp, dusty clouds.

Sadness is a cold, dark cellar
At the bottom of the deep, wet, dark sea.

Sadness is a tree of tears filled with a feeling,
This feeling is sadness.

Natalie Rosie (10)
Fort William RC Primary School, Fort William

Happiness

Happiness is like a waterfall flowing
through your body, enlightening every spirit.

It is a fluffy white cloud, gently raising
you up into the air.

Happiness is a rose swaying in the breeze,
separate from all the other flowers.

Happiness is like a warm day at the beach,
helping you on your way through life.

Jessica MacDonald (11)
Fort William RC Primary School, Fort William

Fun

Fun is red with yellow polka dots.
It tastes like a ton of toffee popcorn
And is the smell of fresh pancakes in the morning.
Fun looks like a motor-powered go-kart just raring to go.
It's the sound of children laughing in the playground
And feels like a never-ending snowball fight.

Calum Davidson Hunter (11)
Fort William RC Primary School, Fort William

Pride

Pride is white, green and yellow
It does not make you cry and it will never make you bellow

Pride tastes like a cake, lovely and round
It feels like a bite of toast just slightly browned

Pride smells like washing powder, lovely and clean
It is a star that will sparkle and gleam

Pride sounds like victory in a lion's roar
It is like a raging young wild boar.

Raymond Munro (10)
Fort William RC Primary School, Fort William

Embarrassment

Embarrassment is red.
It tastes all hot and sticky like fresh toffee straight from the oven.
Embarrassment smells like burning toast.
It looks like cherryade fizzing up inside your stomach,
Spinning like a washing machine.
Embarrassment sounds like a thousand kettles boiling.
It feels like a red-hot fire roaring in your face.
Embarrassment is red.

Taylor Matheson (10)
Fort William RC Primary School, Fort William

Anger

Anger is red like a tomato
And tastes like hot mustard and pepper.
Anger smells like burning rubber
And looks like an erupting volcano.
Anger sounds like a shouting madman
And feels uncontrollable.

Conor Taylor (10)
Fort William RC Primary School, Fort William

Loneliness

Loneliness is a large deserted island,
Its bizarre emptiness saddening our minds.

It is a mountain miles high,
With nobody to enjoy its stunning scenery.

Loneliness is the only cloud in the sky,
With only zooming aeroplanes for company.

It is the only fish in the sea,
About to be trapped in a net.

Nicole Calderwood (10)
Fort William RC Primary School, Fort William

Passion

The colour of passion is a flowing deep red.
It tastes like pancakes with a golden blanket of syrup.
Passion smells as lovely as a red rose.
It sounds like a lovely place with little birds singing in the sun.
Passion feels like people hugging and caring for you.
Passion is warm.
Passion!

Louise Alexander (10)
Fort William RC Primary School, Fort William

Fear

Fear is black, white and grey.
It tastes all dry, like powder and flour.
It smells like rotten eggs
And looks like a dark hall.
Fear sounds like footsteps climbing up the wall
And it feels like snake's skin slithering up your arm.

Savanah Symmers (9)
Fort William RC Primary School, Fort William

Hatred

Hatred is like a raging river,
thrusting the rocks and stones out of its way.

It is dirty dark mud,
squelching and making us fall, gloop, glop, squelch.

Hatred is a cold damp wood,
that makes us shudder and scream.

It is a screeching rock,
hard and hurting everything in its path.

Keira Matheson (11)
Fort William RC Primary School, Fort William

Boredom

Boredom is grey rain clouds.
It tastes like food with no flavour left.
Boredom's smell is stale bread
And looks like an empty room.
Its sound is a clock ticking.
Boredom is waiting.

Connar Mackay (12)
Fort William RC Primary School, Fort William

Playgrounds

P laygrounds are fun
L ittle children playing in the sun
A nd the boys playing with their toys
Y oung children
G iving a hand
R ipping paper and playing with sand
O ur teachers guiding us
U ntil Primary 7
N o one knows what we will do
D octors, nurses, maybe a scientist too!

Shelley Forbes (11)
Foulford Primary School, Fife

Problem Solvers

We are the problem solvers
We're here to help
Just give us a shout or a squeak or a yell
If you fall and scrape your knee or you are stung
By a buzzy wee bee
We'll take you to Mrs Melvin
'Cause she wants to live in harmony

But if I catch you lobbing a punch
You'll be off to see Mrs Allan
Straight after lunch

Problem solvers
They are the best
With our caps
Badges and all the rest

This wouldn't happen without you
Mrs Melvin and Ms Nicholson too!

Marnie Elise Taylor (11)
Foulford Primary School, Fife

Friends

Friends play with you
And you play with them
They make you feel happy
Friends are the best people in the world.

Stewart Leask (7)
Gargunnock Primary School, Stirling

Cakes

I like cakes
Big ones, small ones, tiny ones
Cherry ones, strawberry ones, chocolate ones
But my favourite ones are birthday cakes.

Adam Clayson (7)
Gargunnock Primary School, Stirling

Unicorns

How I love unicorns
They appear once every full moon
Silver all over, including their horns
Flowing mane and tail
They gallop high up into the night
Never to be seen again.

Amy Bruce (8)
Gargunnock Primary School, Stirling

Max

There once was a man called Max
Who could not pay his tax
He was buried alive
Under a hive
And now he is covered in wax.

Scott MacArthur (8)
Gargunnock Primary School, Stirling

Zack

There was a young boy called Zack
Who fell on a steel train track
He jumped in the air
It just wasn't fair
For now he has broken his back.

Andrew Fitches (8)
Gargunnock Primary School, Stirling

Rain

When it is raining
I go inside
And think of something to do
But there's still nothing there
So I do nothing
For the rest of the day.

Colum Blackwood (8)
Gargunnock Primary School, Stirling

Starlight

I think you could come out tonight
I wish we could be friends
For one night, please
Come out tonight
Starlight.

Alistair Petrie (7)
Gargunnock Primary School, Stirling

Mark

There once was a boy called Mark
Who lived in 3 Broom Park
He liked playing games
And called his friends names
But now he is scared of the dark.

Mark Parry (8)
Gargunnock Primary School, Stirling

Snow

Snow!
White, fun
Silver, cold
I love to play in it . . .
Snow.

Alasdair Hyland (8)
Gargunnock Primary School, Stirling

Rain

Rain
Cold, wet
Blue, soggy, falling
Do not go outside!
Rain.

Juliet Jones (8)
Gargunnock Primary School, Stirling

Dogs

Dogs
I like dogs
Because they're furry and soft
And fun to play games with.

Katherine Lewis (8)
Gargunnock Primary School, Stirling

Grace

There was a young girl called Grace
Who couldn't tie a shoelace
She went on the grass
And tripped over some glass
And then she lost the race.

Lucas Jones (8)
Gargunnock Primary School, Stirling

In Space

S pace is very big
P lates will float
A stronauts are one thing that is there
C racked rocks are there as well
E arth is only one planet.

Sam Christie (7)
Gargunnock Primary School, Stirling

If I Had Wings

If I had wings
I would steal some furry white clouds
And feed them to the boiling sun

If I had wings
I would gobble up passing zooming planes
And crunch calmly

If I had wings
I would listen to the people down below
And ask them weird questions

If I had wings
I would smell the scent of fresh bread from underneath me
And while my mouth waters like rain
Think of eating it

If I had wings
I would dream of
Going and touching the green grass
And swimming at the golden seashore.

Sam Ash (8)
Hopeman Primary School, Hopeman

If I Had Wings

If I had wings
I would feel the scorching summer sun
As hot as a white hot flame

If I had wings
I would taste a piece of the fluffy clouds
That feel like sheep's wool

If I had wings
I would listen to the zooming of roller coasters
Faster than cars

If I had wings
I would smell the deep ocean
Which is as fast as snowy days

If I had wings
I would see screeching seals
With bodies of silk

If I had wings
I would dream of jumping over the moon
And touching the stars.

Ellie Hunnybun (9)
Hopeman Primary School, Hopeman

If I Had Wings

If I had wings
I would tenderly stroke the fluffy floating clouds
And glide on the mighty wind

If I had wings
I would nibble miniscule bits of
The moon as nippy as ice cream

If I had wings
I would listen to the cackling of the rain clouds
Drifting on the sapphire-blue sky

If I had wings
I would breathe deep
And sniff the scent of scarlet-red roses

If I had wings
I would stare at the modest people
Who take to the air into cosmos

If I had wings
I would dream of crashing into snow
And diving into the seven seas.

Connor Dunn (8)
Hopeman Primary School, Hopeman

If I Had Wings

If I had wings
I would touch the howling, unstoppable, enormous werewolf
And glide into the middle of the sapphire-blue ocean

If I had wings
I would taste the blood from vampire bats
As cold as the Arctic ice

If I had wings
I would listen to the gigantic dinosaurs' starving wail
As they gaze at the drowsy diplodocus dipping in water

If I had wings
I would breathe in the smell of incredible insects
As they hover above the biggest branch in the universe

If I had wings
I would gaze at the ruby sun
As it falls asleep

If I had wings
I would dream of pouncing on top of a T-Rex
And riding it all the way to blazing, scorching-hot America.

Thomas Collins (8)
Hopeman Primary School, Hopeman

The Heroic Hercules Beetle Is A Warrior

If the Hercules beetle were a warrior
It would be an unbeatable bug,
Marching out in the sunshine,
Gobbling on other mini beasts
Until nightfall
Comes out
And turns into darkness.

Ethan Williams (9)
Hopeman Primary School, Hopeman

Praying Mantis

P retty praying mantis,
R asping at a big juicy bee,
A s fast as a bolt of lightning,
Y anking off its head,
I t makes a lovely snack,
N ibbles it away like bread,
G obbling up some tangy spiders.

M any may attack you,
A s they think you're prey,
N ever go near a luminous mantis,
T errifying it could be,
I f you hear a rustle of leaves,
S tay a distance back!

Daniel Christie (8)
Hopeman Primary School, Hopeman

Ladybirds

L ittle ladybirds fluttering about.
A mazing shells glistening in the sun.
D ashing from leaf to leaf.
Y elling, 'Don't step on me!'
B lack dots.
I nstantly seen.
R uby-red wings.
D azzling in the moonlight.
S campering across the lush green grass.

Cara Main (11)
Hopeman Primary School, Hopeman

If I Had Wings

If I had wings
I would cuddle the softest clouds
And chat to the singing birds

If I had wings
I would taste a super-sized slice
Of the freezing cold moon

If I had wings
I would listen to a croaking frog
In a blazing Amazon river

If I had wings
I would fly to the exotic sun
And wave to a friendly astronaut

If I had wings
I would smell the salty sea air
In every golden beach

If I had wings
I would watch space shuttles
Take off into space
And visit every planet
In the entire blackness of space.

Ross Dick (9)
Hopeman Primary School, Hopeman

Ladybird

L ovely, graceful red and black spotted bug.

A ctively creeping playful bug.

D iamond worth, small and beautiful.

Y ellow and red, we do not even know anymore.

B eautiful bumping bug.

I nspective bug.

R ed and blue bug.

D elicate, rustling bug.

Stuart Gray (8)
Hopeman Primary School, Hopeman

If I Had Wings

If I had wings
I would cuddle the whistling birds
And swoop on the angels' clouds

If I had wings
I would taste a vast slice of the moon
As cold as icy sea

If I had wings
I would hear the howling of the clouds
Whistling that gaze on the white cushions of candy

If I had wings
I would breathe in and out
The scent of raindrops

If I had wings
I would longingly stare at feathery birds
Which grow in the hot yellow sun

If I had wings
I would dream of
Dashing the deserts of hot sand
And swimming in the shark's den.

Shannon East (8)
Hopeman Primary School, Hopeman

Lobster

L imping through the deep sand,
O pening its pincers,
B reaking your hand.
S heds its shell as it grows,
T o make more space, it's like buying new clothes!
E ndless colours like red, yellow, blue,
R acing red creature. *Watch!* it's after you!

Harry Ward (10)
Hopeman Primary School, Hopeman

The Magic Box

(Based on 'Magic Box' by Kit Wright)

I will put in the box . . .
A gold duck in the bright blue sea
The silk of a sparkling dress
An ice cream maker

I will put in the box . . .
A buzzing bee in the fifth season of a black sun
The angel flying up and down
A glittery watch ticking in the box

I will put in the box . . .
The silver flower making a wish
A statue of a pretty princess
The colourful dolphin jumping up and down

I will put in the box . . .
A snowman with a rumbling belly
The butterfly with beautiful wings
A soft teddy bear

My box is fashioned from gold paint,
Silver ghosts hanging from the box
A witch on a broomstick swishing from side to side

I shall dream in the box
In the corner of the box
Then I'd shut my eyes
As black as the night sky.

Anna McPherson (9)
Hopeman Primary School, Hopeman

The Magic Box

(Based on 'Magic Box' by Kit Wright)

I will put in the box . . .
The feather of an intelligent falcon
Delicate melting sand from the scorching deserts
The tip of a holy crumbling mountain

I will put in the box . . .
Strawberry mouth-watering lolly
A giant bite out of a huge chocolate bar
A sip out of a bubbly, delicious milkshake

I will put in the box . . .
A jumping dog and a barking frog
A last flutter of a butterfly
The first crawl of a cuddly cub

I will put in my box . . .
8 days in the week
And a twinkling steaming sun
A Toad with stripes and a Zebra with spots

My box is fashioned from gold and steel
Slithers of money on the lid
And shiny stars in the corners

I will dream in my box
I will swim with squeaking Dolphins
And swim to the golden sand
Then watch the sun go down.

Ashleigh Tripp (8)
Hopeman Primary School, Hopeman

If I Had Wings

If I had wings
I would gently soar up to the breathless heavens
And touch the spectacular dazzle of glamorous angels'
swooshing wings.

If I had wings
I would taste the delicate mouth-watering swish of a
Gorgeous pink summer sunset as hot as a stove on a winter's day.

If I had wings
I would listen to the attractive squeal of a beautiful bottlenose
Dolphin diving and splashing in the shadowy dawn on
the silky sea bed.

If I had wings
I would breathe in the fresh fragrance of a tabby kitten
Purring softly with a special plead

If I had wings
I would gaze sharply with a ferocious flame
In my dazzling eyes

If I had wings
I would dream of waltzing on a desert floor
Shining like the summer sun.

Lauren Oram (8)
Hopeman Primary School, Hopeman

The Magic Box

(Based on 'Magic Box' by Kit Wright)

I will lay in the box . . .
The stench of croaking crickets from a witch's cauldron.
Poison from the tail of a scorching scorpion.
The tip of a tongue touching a tangy mouth-watering grape.

I will lay in the box . . .
Ant-eaters gobbling up grub.
A tip of a wasp's stinger stinging you sharply.
The first half of a centipede stuck to half of a mosquito.

I will bury in the box . . .
Six rough-spoken wishes from a Chinese dragon.
The last snort from a child's laugh
And the first phrase spoken from a snail.

I will place in the box . . .
A fifth season and a dazzling, colourful sun.
A serene Buddha with an ancient knight's shiny sword
And a knight peacefully meditating.

My box is fashioned from blue fire and snakes
With rubies on the lid and demons in the corners.

I shall be a flying belly flopper in my box
On gigantic Mount Everest,
Then land in a field of fluffy cloudy sheep.

Forest Napier (9)
Hopeman Primary School, Hopeman

The Magic Box

(Based on 'Magic Box' by Kit Wright)

I will put in the box . . .
The toot of the last snail on Earth,
The glow from glowing bananas from outer space,
The roughness of a man made from rope.

I will put in the box . . .
A bunch of smoking daisies coughing,
A nibble of fresh fruit from the Amazon rainforest,
A thread from my mum's whiffy socks.

I will put in the box . . .
Three roaring roses roaring in Japanese,
The last whistle from a newborn frog
And the first race of a turtle.

I will put in the box . . .
An eighteenth month and a rainbow dog,
A horse with a collar
And a dog with a saddle.

My box is fashioned from fur and leather and ice,
With dolphins on the lid and jokes in the corners,
Its hinges are singing eagles' toes.

I shall sumo wrestle in my box,
On the top of the remarkable Radnor hills,
Then roly-poly down the fresh green grass
And get covered in grass stains.

Charlotte Ball (9)
Hopeman Primary School, Hopeman

A Magic Box

(Based on 'Magic Box' by Kit Wright)

I will put in my box . . .
The swish of blossom trees on a bright-coloured night
Fresh baked pie on an early spring day
A sip of bouncing water from the freshest lake on land

I will put in my box . . .
A flowing river all the way from roaring Africa
Rushing sea from the gigantic Atlantic
A fierce wind from the whistling highlands

I will put in my box . . .
A polar bear's heart from the top of a pointy mountain
A joyful summer's day from a bright playful park
Wiggly dolphins clapping up and down from the most proud sea

I will put in my box . . .
The first yap from a newborn snugly puppy
A queen in a witch's hat
And a witch in a crown

My box is fashioned from rubies 100 feet long
And bursting flowers in each colourful corner
From evil on the lid and secrets on the walls

I shall dance in my box
In my most dazzling and glamorous dress
On the goldest beach in Hawaii
Then fall asleep under the tallest, greenest palm tree.

Sarah Allanson (11)
Hopeman Primary School, Hopeman

The Seaside Box

(Based on 'Magic Box' by Kit Wright)

I will put in the box . . .
The crash of waves breaking on the scabby rocks.
The magical ice cream van filled with lollipop dreams.
The tiny grains of sand that escape through your fingers
Like burglars from jail.

I will put in the seaside box . . .
The swish of the gentle lapping waves.
A scoop of the creamiest ice cream slowly melting away
On your tongue.
A hungry seagull swooping for its fish dinner.

I will store in my box . . .
Three delighted children jumping over the mini waves.
A picnic hamper filled with mouth-watering sandwiches
And biscuits galore.
Two toddler twins guarding a bucket overflowing with unique shells.

I will put in the box . . .
Yellow sky and blue sand.
A surfer sunbathing and a sunbather surfing.
With socks for gloves and gloves for socks.

My box is fashioned from shells only found at the bottom
Of the silver seas.
With children's laughter on the lid.
Mystical dolphins leaping in the corners.
It is held together with slimy seaweed from the dream ocean.

I shall dive the sea in my box to the glistening seabed
And share the treasures and years of memories
From the seaside box.

Bethannay Grey (9)
Hopeman Primary School, Hopeman

The Super Box

(Based on 'Magic Box' by Kit Wright)

I will put in the box . . .
The pop of a perfect party balloon
A fragment of ice from crimson Mars
The touch of an angry ant

I will put in the box . . .
The heroic sight of a thumping T-Rex
The sonic laughter of a humorous hyena
An eraser that can write
And a pencil that can erase

I will put in the box . . .
My mad mum moaning moodily at Mark's party
A fridge of flaming fire
And a stove of sub-zero cold

I will put in my box . . .
A smell of a fried fish in the sweltering Sahara desert,
A taste of a bean plant which makes peas
A madman who isn't mad

My box is fashioned from desiccated bones from the greatest warriors
And blunt swords remaining from the mightiest dragon slayers
And the biggest celebrities' faces on the glacial lid
New gold on the old corners and the hinges are made from tattered
tigers' tails

I will wrestle in my box
In the biggest ring in the Milky Way
And do my mega move . . .
1, 2, 3!

Thomas Johnson (10)
Hopeman Primary School, Hopeman

The Magic Box

(Based on 'Magic Box' by Kit Wright)

I will put in my box . . .
The swish of the grandest forest in the dead of night
The fresh blossoms from the angels above
A mouth-watering melon touching my slimy tongue

I will put in my box . . .
A snow angel singing enchantingly to the dancing snowflakes
A sip of water from the glimmering sea
A leaping splash from a mystical dolphin

I will put in my box . . .
Three secret wishes my nana last told me
The last breath of my great grandad
And the first smile from a fluffy kitten

I will put in my box . . .
A newborn baby and the golden sun
A fish in a swimming pool
And people in a fish tank

My box is fashioned with diamonds and rubies
With love in the air and kisses in the corner
Its hinges are the rings of kings and queens

I shall shop in my box
In the grandest shops in New York
Then drive in the largest limo in the world
Then fall back into my dreams.

Kathrin Munday (10)
Hopeman Primary School, Hopeman

The Magic Box

(Based on 'Magic Box' by Kit Wright)

I will put in my box . . .
The everlasting clear blue sea clashing against the dazzling shore,
The swishing of the palm trees in the breezy wind
The sail rising in the bold beautiful sunset

I will put in my box . . .
The gorgeous golden sand chilling out
The twinkle of the clear blue sea
The textures of the great big leaves like wax on your fingers

I will put in my box . . .
The smell of the salty sea
The scent of newly-baked fish
The sweat of hardworking people

I will put in my box . . .
The mouth-watering juicy watermelon
The flavour of a bristly coconut
The taste of the fantastic fish

My box is covered in chocolate kisses
The hinges in midget gems
The lock the dream and secrets I know

Lastly, I will put in my box . . .
The touch of people's souls I will always remember.

Ailie Robertson (11)
Hopeman Primary School, Hopeman

My Fantasy Box

(Based on 'Magic Box' by Kit Wright)

I will shove in my box . . .
The mighty rough roar of a thrilling tiger on the deepest sunset,
Glacial icicles from the blast of a wintry frost dragon,
The sweltering sun above my aching head.

I will place in my box . . .
A mystic centaur with a jumpy stomach,
A ferocious dragon of water
And a legendary hydra of fire.

I will shove in my box . . .
Magical monkeys swinging cheerfully through lollipop trees,
Dirty dinosaurs rampaging through the vulnerable village,
A joking jackal growling murderously.

My box is fashioned with rigid ogre horns,
With puffy clouds on the lid and whispering winds in the corners,
The hinges are the joints of a caveman's leg.

I shall fly in my mysterious box,
Over the shining moon,
Then land on the highest mountain,
The colour of the shimmering stars.

Corin Smith (10)
Hopeman Primary School, Hopeman

In The Playground

Friends are fighting
Boys are bullying
Ellie is eating
Fred is falling
Susan is skipping
Ben is bored
Josh is jolly
This is how we feel
And what we do in the playground.

Hannah Foubister (8)
Kellands School, Inverurie

People Playing

Darren's playing football
Robbie's playing too
Emily's skipping
Katie's laughing
Benny's shouting, 'Hair!'

Tommy's making mess
Becky's shouting, 'Yeah!'
Tom is playing Star Wars
John is playing guns
George is playing cars

Harry's hurt
Matt's not
Tessa's jolly
Playing with
Best friend, Tess.

Clair Binnie (10)
Kellands School, Inverurie

Wrestling Night

It comes on a Monday night,
Randy Orton, what a sight!
The Rockers get kicked out of the ring
By Jim Ross and The King.
A choke-slam by Kane,
The powers of pain go out with crash,
Chris Master says he's never been beat,
But Kane says, 'You're dead meat!'
A big drop-kick by Triple H,
Rosie goes out with a big *slam!*
Ding! Ding! Ding! End of the match,
Batista wins, what a thrash.

Jamie Dow (12)
Kellands School, Inverurie

Girls Rule, Boys Drool

Boys hit and bite,
Girls sing and fight,
Listening to the wind.

The boys say girls
Are so moany,
The girls say boys
Are so gory.
The sun has gone,
Bye-bye,
So long.

Maia Stanton (9)
Kellands School, Inverurie

Friends In The Playground

F red is friendly
R oss is rushing!
I mogen is excited!
E llen is telling!
N atasha is nudging!
D uncan is drawing!

Harriet Paterson (9)
Kellands School, Inverurie

Actions In The Playground

Morven's dancing
Kirsty's prancing
Penny's shouting
I am bouncing
Karen's moaning
Sandra's posing
Erin's rich
Jill's a titch.

Louise O'Rourke (8)
Kellands School, Inverurie

In The Playground

In the playground girls
skip around.

In the playground boys
muck around.

In the playground teachers
look around.

In the playground no one
frowns!

Rosalind Watt (9)
Kellands School, Inverurie

One By One

One by one children sing
Two by two children swing
Three by three children fall
Four by four kids kick balls
Five by five kids hit a hive
Six by six bees are alive
Seven by seven kids are late
Eight by eight they're in a state
Nine by nine they're in a line
Ten by ten none look fine.

Kirstin Mitchell (8)
Kellands School, Inverurie

Playground

1, 2, don't like you
3, 4, girls dancing
5, 6, girls skipping
7, 8, take a break
9, 10, let's do it again.

Struan Cruickshank (9)
Kellands School, Inverurie

In The Playground

Robert's rushing
Daniel's crushing
Kayleigh's crying
Sarah's skipping
William's waiting
James is jumping
Rebecca's racing
Harry is hopping
Graham's grumpy
And Darren's touching *hair!*

Phillip Woodgreaves (8)
Kellands School, Inverurie

In The Playground

In the playground
Fred is fighting
Sandy is sleeping
Benny is bored
Matthew is marking
Rebecca is reading
Sam is sliding
Fiona is falling
But me, I am pulling
Hair!

David Biddle (9)
Kellands School, Inverurie

1-10

1, 2, tie my shoe
3, 4, knock on a door
5, 6, football tricks
7, 8, through the gate
9, 10, found a pen.

Jason Banks (8)
Kellands School, Inverurie

In The Playground

Daniel is dancing
Paul is prancing
Greg is glancing
Sandra is singing
Barry is bouncing
Craig is crying
Bradley is bullying
And Stuart is shouting.

Ben Rattray (9)
Kellands School, Inverurie

Playground Fun

Greg is playing football
Bradley is playing too
Alex is laughing
Aimee is skipping

Penny is screaming
Jay is running
Lois is splashing in puddles
Ellen is picking up litter
Emily is too.

Orianne Watt (10)
Kellands School, Inverurie

Rhyme To Ten

1, 2, what to do.
3, 4, at the door.
5, 6, play with Ben.
7, 8, now we're late.
9, 10, to the den!

Tony Wishart (9)
Kellands School, Inverurie

Bad Manners

1, 2, steal a shoe
3, 4, slam a door
5, 6, make a mess
7, 8, be a pest
9, 10, do it again.

Sean Mayberry (9)
Kellands School, Inverurie

Why Me?

Why do they pick on me?
Why do they start on me?
Why can't they plant a tree
Instead of picking on me?
Why me?

Calum Yule (9)
Kellands School, Inverurie

The Playground

The playground is my favourite place
It really has a lot of space
You can run about
Scream and shout
Because we are free!
When the bell goes
We're all in
Doing work
It's such a sin
It rings again
We're having fun
The playground is number
One!

Sarah-Jane Sawdon (8)
Kildrum Primary School, Cumbernauld

The Day The Flying Saucer Came!

The day the flying saucer came,
We thought it was a Frisbee,
The boys didn't mind,
They weren't interested,
But us girls, we were,
We threw it up,
We threw it down,
We threw it all around,
Until eventually it came down.
It hit the ground with a real *smack!*
We ran for it but it didn't come back,
A boy came with his bike,
He stood on it and snapped it hard,
He picked it up and threw it hard,
It hit the puddle with a *crack!*
We looked at it staring back,
Hoping it would soon come back.

Sophie Cavanagh (8)
Kildrum Primary School, Cumbernauld

Playtime

Get your play piece out,
All rush out,
The playground is like a pot of gold,
Sparkly, shiny, clean and bold.
Berries on the trees like beads
And the sweet smell of sweets,
Crunching, munching of the apple core,
Get a ball and play some more.
We all adore the ladybirds
And lots more.
I love the noise of the girls and boys,
Screaming, shouting, making noise,
Then, *bring! bring!* We all go in.

Kirsty Deakin (8)
Kildrum Primary School, Cumbernauld

Playtime Is Cool

A, B, C,
1, 2, 3,
Bell rings,
Race to the swings.
They're all full,
Start to pull.
Skipping ropes out,
Fun all about,
We're glad
But John's being bad.
There's a sound,
Rock the ground.
There's a blow,
We all know,
Time to go in,
Rubbish in the bin.

Chelsea Tominey (9)
Kildrum Primary School, Cumbernauld

Playtime

P is for the playground that gets tidied every day.
L is for listening to everyone bawling.
A is for arguing in the autumn breeze.
Y is for yelling every single day.
T is for telling kids to behave.
I is for interesting things to play.
M is for murals upon the wall.
E is for enjoying playtime every day.

Ruth McCutcheon (9)
Kildrum Primary School, Cumbernauld

Playtime

Girls giggle
Boys shout
Everybody run about
Balls bang
Hands clap
Bullies slap
Me on the back
Girls scream
In fright
When the boys
Start to fight
Teachers pull
Out their hair
When we use
The ground
As chairs
Ding! Ding!
Time up
Callum shouts
'Just my luck!'
We all know what
It means
No more playtime
For you and me.

Emma McIntosh (8)
Kildrum Primary School, Cumbernauld

The Playground

The sun is shining
All about
Boys and girls
Come barging out
People fall and
People call
All the people have a ball
The trees are swaying
To and fro
In the winter we catch the flu
Girls are gossiping
Boys have fights
Let's go out
We have light
The plants are growing
One at a time
We can look there's no more grime!
We can shout
We can scream
Everybody has a dream!

Emma Henderson (9)
Kildrum Primary School, Cumbernauld

The Playground

Girls giggle
Boys shout
Bullies come
Barging out
The sound of children
All around
Fun never ends
In the playground
Eat your bun
Eat your crisps
Just get it done
Before *bring, bring!*
Get in!
So throw wrappers
In the bin
Bullies get their
Last kick before
The teacher's mean
'In! In! In!'

Kayleigh Tominey (9)
Kildrum Primary School, Cumbernauld

An Hour Out Of School

An hour out of school,
In the summer sun,
I trek through dangerous grounds,
How's that for number one?

It's lunchtime and I'm still going,
Animals are common,
Six or eight legs and little bodies,
They creep out us women!

As I walk past something,
I wonder what it is,
Then I realise it's a jungle gym,
I'm smart to notice this!

The wind is getting stronger,
The trees are getting wilder,
This holiday is quite a handful,
The weather could have been milder.

I can hear the idols singing,
Far, far away,
They sound quite young though,
Maybe that's their way.

Oops, that's the bell!
I better get out of the playground.

Melanie Robinson (11)
Kininmonth Primary School, Peterhead

My Best Friend

Deon is a very good friend
We became friends on a bus
I sat beside him
We started chatting, now we are friends

Deon is a very good athlete
He supports Aberdeen FC
He is in the Kininmonth School football team
Deon is brilliant at football

Deon has blond hair
And is very small
He has blue eyes
And has a lot of freckles

Deon is very funny
He is very chatty
And is sometimes stupid
Deon is crazy

Deon loves chips
His favourite food is lasagne
He likes Chinese food
And he likes a kebab

Deon is my best friend.

Shane McDonald (11)
Kininmonth Primary School, Peterhead

Jade

Jade is very cuddly because she sits on my knee.
She is really cute.
She is black, white and brown.
Jade hates fighting with Rocky.

Jade likes to eat.
She likes to drink.
She likes getting cuddles.
She is really furry.

She doesn't like the vet.
She doesn't like the car.
She doesn't like anyone sharing her bed.
She barks when she is hungry or when she hears things.

She is very friendly.
Jade is very nice and happy.
She is very nosy.
Jade is very sweet and soft.

Suzann McDonald (11)
Kininmonth Primary School, Peterhead

Planet Blig Blag Blog

In Planet Blig Blag Blog
The grass is very red,
The houses are made of sweets
And the trees are black as lead.

The cutlery dances,
People are blue blobs.
Animals are white,
All they eat is Hobnobs.

On Planet Blig Blag Blog,
All you smell is sweets.
If you didn't know,
Chocolate lines the streets.

Sophie Payne (10)
Kininmonth Primary School, Peterhead

The Widow's World

The widow comes out the creepy church,
Surrounded by a swirling mist.
The life of Mary Churchill
Had an evil twist.

40 years of happiness,
40 years of joy,
3 years after marriage
They had a baby boy,
They were married at 25,
But only one is now alive.

The happiness ended on a scary night,
The sound that was heard,
Gave Mary a fright,
So she went out,
To see what it was all about.
She looked all around
And then she found,
Her husband, dead on the ground.

Mary had a long cry
And thought,
How could somebody watch him die?
Why did someone show such hate
And why did this person decide his fate?

3 days later,
She went to the undertaker,
But when she went in the door,
She couldn't take it,
That her husband wasn't alive anymore.

So widow Mary Churchill,
Wondering about life
And 2 weeks ago,
She was a wife.

Patterson Gough (11)
Kininmonth Primary School, Peterhead

Puzzle

Puzzle is my auntie's pet pony,
She does not like to be lonely,
Puzzle likes to be ridden
And she likes to jump in the midden.

Puzzle is very friendly and quiet
And would never start a big riot,
Puzzle's coat is sandy gold
And always does what she is told.

She likes to be brushed
And her food to be mushed,
She likes to be sprayed with a hose
But hates water up her nose.

Puzzle is a perfect pony
And hates to walk on a beach that is stony,
I wish she was mine,
So I could play with her all the time.

Jacquie Leel (11)
Kininmonth Primary School, Peterhead

Fraser

Fraser is a kind person,
He helps me with problems,
He is a bit of a joker,
Fraser is forgiving.

Fraser plays football,
He has dark blond hair,
You can talk to him about things,
He is my best friend.

Fraser can keep secrets,
He lives on a farm,
We've been friends for six years,
Fraser plays for the football team.

Paul Murray (11)
Kininmonth Primary School, Peterhead

Shane

My best friend is very funny,
We were friends since the first day we met,
He is brill at football
And we've been friends ever since.

My best friend is crazy about Rangers FC,
He also likes tandoori and Chinese foods.
He is a very good friend to have,
He's got loads of freckles.

My best friend has nine brothers and sisters,
We both love chips,
He likes Lord of the Rings,
He is very whacky.

My best friend is very fast,
He is the goalkeeper
For Kininmonth School,
My best friend is Shane.

Deon Allen (11)
Kininmonth Primary School, Peterhead

Crystal

Crystal is my 13.2hh pony
She hates being lonely
Crystal's a 27-year-old mare
Her fur is grey but her mane is fair

Crystal loves to be groomed
When she sees you, she'll start to zoom
Right over to you to get her food
Crystal is very good

Her favourite food is sugar-beet
If she eats too much, she'll get sore feet
She likes oats just as good
But grass is there when she's got no food.

Meggie Gough (10)
Kininmonth Primary School, Peterhead

The Beach

Packing sunscreen,
We're going to the beach!
Packing swimming costumes,
We're going to the beach!

We got in the car,
We're going to the beach!
Shoved in our luggage,
We're going to the beach!

Dashed to the beach,
We're going to the beach.
Unpacked our things,
We're going to the beach!

Sunbathed in the sun,
We're going to the beach!
Got a crab in my pants,
We're going to the beach!

Had a swim in the sea,
We're going to the beach!
Had a bite to eat,
We're going to the beach!

Packed up our things,
We've been to the beach!
Drove back home,
We've been to the beach!

Got out the car,
We've been to the beach!
Unpacked our luggage,
I want to go again!

Alastair Robinson (10)
Kininmonth Primary School, Peterhead

My Favourite Something

My favourite thing,
Maybe something big,
Something small or
Something in the middle.

My favourite thing,
Maybe something fat,
Something thin or
Something in the centre.

My favourite thing,
Maybe something to do,
It's maybe me,
It's maybe you.

My favourite thing,
I'm not sure what it is,
My favourite thing
Is probably this.

Alexandra Abbott (11)
Kininmonth Primary School, Peterhead

Cats

Cats are really cute,
they like playing all the time.
Cats come small and big,
but they don't come wearing wigs.
I wish all the cats were mine.

You get lots of cats,
it's a shame they don't wear hats.
Cats, cats are so cute,
it's a shame they can't wear suits.
That's the end of my cat poem.

Louise MacGregor (9)
Longforgan Primary School, Longforgan

Big And Small

When I was one
A box looked like an endless pit
The door looked like a portal to another world
And I felt small

When I was three
A TV screen looked like a cinema screen
It looked like a scrap heap of metal
I felt tiny

When I was five
A book looked like a load of paper
The cat looked like a proud lion
I felt frightened

When I was seven
A box looked like a box
And the door looked like a door
I felt tall

When I was nine
A TV screen looked like a TV screen
The car looked like a car
I felt huge

Now I am eleven
Everything looks how it is
And it is normal . . . for now.

Alexander Hayes (11)
Longforgan Primary School, Longforgan

When I Was . . .

When I was one
A cupboard was a dark cave,
The bath was as big as the ocean
And I felt scared.

When I was three
My dad was a giant,
The sofa was a huge mountain
And I felt small.

When I was five
Primary sevens were fierce monsters,
The light was like the sun
And I felt frightened.

When I was seven
Mrs McArthy was a lion,
A rhino was as big as a car
And I felt taller.

When I was nine
My friends were like angels,
The primary sevens were less like monsters
And I felt fine.

Now I'm eleven
A sofa is a sofa,
A rhino is a rhino
And I feel tall.

Callum Fowlie (11)
Longforgan Primary School, Longforgan

All About Me!

Once upon a time
there was a fantastic girl
who was called Caitlin

She was 9 years old
she really liked fast dancing
she loved football too

She liked the colours
black and purple very much
this was about me.

Caitlin Fowlie (9)
Longforgan Primary School, Longforgan

Space

A big rocket launched
above the Earth into space,
see the planet Earth.

See the moon and Mars
and the gas ball, Jupiter
and the silver moon.

Daniel Davidson (9)
Longforgan Primary School, Longforgan

The Gargoyles

In an old temple
I saw lots of weird gargoyles
I was petrified

They were furious
They wanted to attack me
But they were just stone!

Melissa Lonie (9)
Longforgan Primary School, Longforgan

Trains

Trains are wonderful,
trains are very, very fast,
trains are really fun.

Trains are amazing,
trains go under dark tunnels,
trains carry people.

Virgin is the best,
First are better than Virgin,
they can go up hills.

Trains are so brilliant,
trains come in big and tiny,
trains are massive things.

Ray Lynham (9)
Longforgan Primary School, Longforgan

Dancing

When I came in today
I heard the music thumping,
I saw my friends swishing,
Swirling and laughing.
I . . .
Twirled to the mats,
Where the people were.
I smelled the perfume
From the dance teacher.
I wanted to dance
To the music,
Jumping up and down
And doing high kicks all around.
After it was all done
We pranced to the changing rooms
And I thought,
Great, I've just learnt a new dance.

Shannon Shields (10)
McGill Primary School, Glasgow

The Gymnast

There he is in the pits,
Stretching out in the splits,
There she is on the beam,
While the coach is
Coaching the trampoline.

He was swinging on the hoops,
Then he flipped
Right through the springboard,
She is running for the springboard,
She jumps, it creaks,
Then the trampoline squeaks.

Little Wendy is really trendy,
Don't get me wrong, she's really bendy,
Her leotard is glittering and glossy,
Her coach is also really bossy.

Her competition is on Thursday,
She'll flip, better not trip,
Her hair will shimmer in the light,
She's gonna try with all her might,
She's so excited,
As her mum's invited.

Stuart Beveridge (11)
McGill Primary School, Glasgow

Running

Every person lining up waiting
To get up and off
On the starting block
Nervous, shaking
Talking from the crowd
The race is on
Everyone an individual
Running to and fro
Competitors wondering if they'll
Get bronze, silver or gold!
Rubber burning beneath their feet
Needing all the power they've got
To seek a first?
A second
Or a third?

Hitting a stitch
You're slowing down
About to burst, you're going down
One person is in the lead
'Hooray,' she shouts
The finish line is about now
It's right in front of her
She snaps the ribbon - she's won!
The people shout, 'Hooray, hooray!
You've won, now it's all over.'

Dale Carroll (9)
McGill Primary School, Glasgow

Swimming Fun

Happy, excited, swimming fun,
People talking all day long.
Some chlorine in the water,
People jump in with a splash.

Shouting and squealing
As you go down the chute,
Hot or cold,
Have fun while we are there,
When we are going to the showers,
Shampoo smells too
And bubbles going up your nose.

Me and you having fun,
Some people happy, some sad,
Some can't swim and that is bad!

Amy Brown (10)
McGill Primary School, Glasgow

Dancing

I want to twirl and swirl to the music
Jumping up and down
I love to dance because it makes me
Feel free from the bad things
I can't wait to get there
It's brilliant to dance
I'm there - I still can't wait
I want to twirl and swirl to the music
Jumping up and down
I danced to the left
I danced to the right
I went round and round
Till the stars came out at night
I can't wait till next time
Hooray, hooray.

Emma McArthur (9)
McGill Primary School, Glasgow

Dodge Ball

Running round the small gym hall
Trying not to get hit with the ball
People running by, screaming
No time for daydreaming
Be aware, don't stare
In the middle of nowhere
Always running, don't look back
Or you could be in for a healthy smack
If you're hit, you will have to sit
And that's the end of it
There is no break, you're at stake
Running out of puff
And if you do
That's just tough
Smash, smack, crunch
What an unlucky bunch
Sore faces, balls in all places
Gym's up for today
Thank goodness it wasn't me.

John Chaudhry (11)
McGill Primary School, Glasgow

Cheerleading Is My Best Thing *Ever!*

Up in the sky, the flyers are high,
The pink and black suits are very, very cute,
The team is cool as we stand on our stools and shout!
I hear calling from the stands,
The team and me feel happy and cheery,
I smell coffee and tea from the crowd,
My friend is a flyer and she flies high.

Rebecca Lees (10)
McGill Primary School, Glasgow

The Magic Box

(Based on 'Magic Box' by Kit Wright)

My box is made of diamonds,
Pink and blue fur and a golden sun,
Stuck on the side of my box will be a lovely soft teddy.

In my box I shall put . . .
All my happy memories I've had with my family,
All the good times I've had with my friends
And all the bad times I've had with my friends.

In my box I will have . . .
Dogs, cats, puppies and kittens rolling around,
I will also put hundreds of people dancing
And falling in love under the heavens above,
Also all the beautiful gardens in the world.

In my box I will put . . .
All my cuddly teddies
I cuddle at night.

Lisa McLauchlan (11)
McGill Primary School, Glasgow

Fast Cars

The fast car starts,
The sub car neon glows.
The gunfire bangs
And away we go,
He checks his mirror,
What does he see?
Flashing blue lights,
The colour of the sea.
The cops shouting,
'Stop your vehicle!'
'Why should I?
I didn't even get that far!'

Daniel Kelly (9)
McGill Primary School, Glasgow

Street Race

Amazing cars lined up at the start
A dodge charger raring to race
The deserted streets
With their challenging bends
Is the perfect place for a midnight street race
The Honda s2000 with its 20-inch chrome rims
Every performance upgrade imaginable on it
The Audi TT's noisy exhaust echoing the streets
The Nissan pulses carbon fibre spoiler
And roof scoop sped the car up by far
The eager crowd cheered them on
3, they had their feet glued to the pedal
2, their hearts were pounding furiously
1, it sped away from the finish line
The crowd was roaring
All that was visible was a black puff of smoke
The 4 cars sped around the corners, not braking at all
The dodge charger taking the lead
Flying around the roundabout at 120mph
The Audi TT at the back
Pushed the nitro and went zooming past
The dodge charger
Coming up a drawbridge, came into sight
The dodge shot up behind the TT and when they were
Coming up the drawbridge
The charger went over the TT
And landed with ease
Passed the finish line and took the cash.

Gavin Docherty (11)
McGill Primary School, Glasgow

Car Race

Starting on the start line
Engines roaring, neon's pulsing
14-inch amps
Tunes blaring
Off they go!

Halfway up the deserted street
Body-kit scrapped and scraped
Smelling the burning tyres
Beaming out the backfire
Pulling up to second place
Smack!
Chrome rim fell off
I am tempted to press NOS button
And I flew so fast like a cheetah
I went supersonic
Went past first place
I was going at a pace
I went straight past the finish line
The crowd was blaring.

Lee McLuckie (11)
McGill Primary School, Glasgow

Street Racing

The guns go
The cars go
Like a flash they go
Round the bend
With a lot of the cars
Going into the barrier
The rest go like
Lightning
Up the hill
With Bill
Falling behind
With Lee leading
The race is about to end
It is a photo finish
And we have a winner . . .
James Lawson
About to open a bottle of champagne
There he is, lifting the cup
We have our 2005
Street racing winner!

David Dawson (10)
McGill Primary School, Glasgow

Gymnastics

I can see the colourful leotards
The gymnasts are wearing
While they are glaring
Round the corner to see the flips
Which they are doing in the pits

I feel sweaty on the beam
While I am waiting for my theme
And people on the trampoline

I can also smell the rubber of mats
While the girl does her acrobats
The girl moves gracefully along the floor
Jumping, twirling, leaping, we want more

My competition was last week
My little sister was playing hide-and-seek

I had to go a little walk
And rub my hands in the chalk
While I was there the mats were bare
So I share my expressions in the air.

Amy McLachlan (9)
McGill Primary School, Glasgow

Gymnastics

I can see people bouncing on big trampolines,
I can hear my friend laughing
As she runs across the room,
After I've done my *groovy mushroom*
I do my bends and I do my very hard stretches.
I feel very tired and hungry,
Suddenly crowds went very quiet
And music went wild
And the gymnastic girls came flying out.
My friend and me were running out to the stage.
We were performing on the stage,
We were springing on trampolines
And doing handstands on the beam.
After the trials we all sat down
For the big moment,
We sat down on the floor
And waited for the trophies,
The announcer yelled out our name
And we were screaming like mad.
We got our trophy and took a good bow
And we all went home.

Samantha Gorrell (11)
McGill Primary School, Glasgow

Baseball Glory

The sweat dripped onto the ground
As I looked from player to player.
Suddenly it went silent,
You could hear a small pin drop.

The ball glided through the air like a glider,
As it came it went quiet,
The ball came tumbling
Towards me as if in slow motion,
You could almost hear
The wind from the ball and *whack!*
The sound of the ball
Hitting off the bat
Was like a gunshot or a hammer
Against metal,
You could hear everyone gasp.

During that time all the guilt came back
Because of that whack we could lose.
It landed!
Simultaneously my fellow players and I sprinted,
Dodged from stumps,
Hearts beating incredibly fast.

The crowd shouting, screaming, 'Faster,
Faster, come on!'
Stop, it was over!

Our team won,
The other team were depressed,
But we were ready for a rest!

Janice Buchanan (10)
McGill Primary School, Glasgow

My Senses

The bells were ringing in the town centre
And everyone was listening
I can see the hailstones
Smacking off my windowpane
I can smell the polish
Left sitting on the fireplace
I love the taste of sour sweets
In the jar in the sweetie shop
I love to touch my glass windows
Every time I'm going out.

Jordan Stewart (9)
Mosspark Primary School, Glasgow

A Sense Poem

I can hear the bells ringing,
Calling people to church.
I can see my school,
Where we go to work.
I can smell the smoke,
Barbeques that I love.
I can taste my dinner,
Fish fingers and chips.
I love to touch Lottie
A soft little dog that comes into my garden to play.

Jonathan McInulty (7)
Mosspark Primary School, Glasgow

Sea

The waves grow, tides are low
Beautiful to watch, glow
The sea is glinting.

Maryam Raza (7)
Mosspark Primary School, Glasgow

My Senses

Outside I hear the banging
Of the drum next door.

I love to see my baby sister jiggle
When I jump up and say, *'Boo!'*

I love the smell of cooking
And knowing my dinner's nearly ready.

I love to taste a McDonald's
It is so good.

I love to touch my baby sister
Her skin is so soft.

Reiss Callaghan (8)
Mosspark Primary School, Glasgow

My Senses

The sound that I love to hear
Is a match at Parkhead.

I look at fireworks
How beautiful the sparks are.

The taste I love
Is sugary tea at my gran's.

I love the smell of petrol
From a garage full of cars.

I love the feel of a new rubber
With a lovely bright colour.

Chad Meechan (8)
Mosspark Primary School, Glasgow

My Senses

I hear people clapping
When I walk down the street.

I see the sunset
As it shines down on the world.

I can smell a rotting banana
Lying by the bin.

I love the taste of ice cream
When it is a sunny day.

I love the soft pillow
When I am warm in my bed.

Amy Gow (8)
Mosspark Primary School, Glasgow

Senses

I hear the sound of music
Right from my CD player

I can see the sunset
In the blazing sky

I love the smell of petrol
It reminds me of my old car

I touch my teddy bear
It's fluffy as a cloud

The sweet taste of ice cream
Is like Heaven in my mouth.

Jacob Collins (8)
Mosspark Primary School, Glasgow

Senses

The sound of animals in the zoo
Is the sound of my class at playtime!

Look at the sunset up in the sky
With its lovely bright colours.

I love the smell of paint
It makes the house smell so fresh.

I love to touch fur
So soft and cuddly.

The sour taste in my mouth
Swells up my jaws!

Lucy Mathieson (8)
Mosspark Primary School, Glasgow

Senses

I can hear birds singing
As they fly above the clouds.
I see a little baby
Growing up to be beautiful.
I love the smell of petrol
When I am at the airport.
I love vanilla ice cream
When I am very hot.
I love the fluffy feel of my pillow
So relaxing to sleep on.

Gary Hannah (8)
Mosspark Primary School, Glasgow

Sea

A starfish swims on dry land
Beaming, dreaming like the sea
The ocean is magic.

Rebecca McIlroy (7)
Mosspark Primary School, Glasgow

Love

Love smells like lovely roses,
On a beautiful summer's day,
Love reminds me of cherubs in the sky,
Flying so high!
Love is the colour of baby pink,
So soft and cuddly,
Love looks like fluffy cushions,
Puffy and pretty!
Love tastes like sweet candyfloss,
Melting in your mouth,
Love sounds like soft harps!
Playing away,
Love feels like your heart's on cloud nine!

Ashley Ross (10)
Newcastle Primary School, Glenrothes

John

There was a young boy called John,
Who got bit by a massive swan,
He ran shouting, 'Mum,
Look at my thumb.'
His mum said, 'Oh, be quiet, John.'

Darren Wallace (12)
Newcastle Primary School, Glenrothes

The Man With Hair Like A Bear

There was an old man that was drunk,
He spent the whole night in a trunk,
It messed up his hair,
He looked like a bear!
Now he doesn't sleep in a trunk.

Joanne Kelly (10)
Newcastle Primary School, Glenrothes

My Cat

A little kitten,
As small as a mitten.

A comfort giver,
A long liver.

A good pet,
As small as a net.

A big eater,
A long sleeper.

A bundle of joy,
As tiny as a toy.

Any guesses what it is?
It's my little cat!

Danielle Sweeney (11)
Newcastle Primary School, Glenrothes

Sadness

It tastes like water
But it's saltier!
It feels like a raindrop
Sliding down your cheek!
It is clear,
Like an empty bottle of beer!
It reminds me of rain
That falls from the clouds!
It sounds like the sea,
It makes you want a cup of tea!
It smells like saliva,
The saliva that wanders in your mouth!
It looks like rain
That dissolves in the sun!

Nadya Glen (12)
Newcastle Primary School, Glenrothes

Fear!

Fear is dark, fear is sad,
Fear is a scientist gone completely mad.
Fear is dark, fear is mean,
Keep saying to yourselves, *it's only a dream.*
Fear is dark and unforgiving,
Thank the Lord that you're still living.
Fear is dark, fear is fine,
Fear sends shivers down your spine.
Fear is dark, fear is a key,
I see you, but you don't see me!

Kirstie Sinclair (11)
Newcastle Primary School, Glenrothes

Silly Bill

There once was a man called Bill,
That died and left a will,
He left his house
To an old field mouse
And his car to a cat called Phil.

Caitlin Collins (11)
Newcastle Primary School, Glenrothes

Bill

There was an old man called Bill,
Who forgot to take his pill,
He threw a fit
And fell in a pit,
That silly old man called Bill.

Andrew Bathie (11)
Newcastle Primary School, Glenrothes

I Think My Teacher Is A Superhero!

It's not just that she drives a car with gadgets in every pocket!
It's not just that she comes to school wearing a mask and a cape!
It's not just that she calls the headteacher's office the
                                        police headquarters!
It's not just that she flies to the teacher's lounge every break!
It's that she shouts . . .
'Super teacher to the rescue!'
Every time someone gets hurt!

Emma Fotheringham (11)
Newcastle Primary School, Glenrothes

Hate!

Hate smells like sticky tar drying out on a hot day.
It tastes like very hot chilli peppers burning in my mouth.
It looks like bullies hurting and battering a child.
It feels like eating the coldest ice cream on Earth.
It sounds like people banging on the drums as loud as they can.
It reminds me of horrible people fighting and punching the poor.
Hate is the colour of black, like my mind going blank!

Kirsten Elder (11)
Newcastle Primary School, Glenrothes

Love

It looks like red love hearts floating in the sky.
It sounds like wine glasses banging together.
It smells like roses and carnations.
It tastes like Thorntons' ice cream.
It reminds me of wedding rings.
Red is the colour of love!

Samantha Gibson (11)
Newcastle Primary School, Glenrothes

Hate

It sounds like a kettle bubbling in my head.
It reminds me of getting clawed by an eagle,
With the blood dripping from my arm.

Blue is the colour of hate, like a cold winter's morning
With no heat left in you.

It smells like the ash of a burnt-out fire,
Like a cigarette left to burn in the night.

It tastes like a bowl of dry porridge,
Like the taste of an apple that's rotten.

It looks like a match that's lit a fire
Making a blaze that will destroy.

It feels like a stake ripping through my heart.

Craig Hutchison (11)
Newcastle Primary School, Glenrothes

Johnny

There was a bonnie boy called Johnny,
The girls thought he was very funny,
He got picked for the team,
His ball rolled into the stream,
The lucky big boy called Johnny.

Alastair Wallace (12)
Newcastle Primary School, Glenrothes

Kirstie Custard

There once was a girl called Kirstie Custard,
Who slipped on a patch of mustard.
She fell with a whack
And broke her back,
That silly girl called Kirstie Custard.

Melissa Paul (11)
Newcastle Primary School, Glenrothes

Father

1964 dad, is good at his job, a policeman.
He'll arrest you if you're bad,
He's a number one dad.
With dark hair and blue eyes,
He'll catch you by surprise.
Might need a wee repair,
He'll always take care.
Offers start at £3000.

Lauren McLeod (11)
Newcastle Primary School, Glenrothes

Hallowe'en!

Spooky!
Trick or treaters,
People having some fun!
Skeletons hanging from the ceiling,
Scared yet?

Louise Wallace (10)
Newcastle Primary School, Glenrothes

Fear

Fear feels like butterflies in your stomach,
Fear smells like rotten eggs in a haunted house,
Fear sounds like someone getting murdered in the woods,
Fear smells like *blood* and *guts,*
Fear reminds you of a black cat with yellow eyes,
Fear is red like the Devil,
Fear looks like the *Grudge!*

Sarah Mann (11)
Newcastle Primary School, Glenrothes

Summer

The birds are playing
The sweet little things in the sun
They are having so much fun
I guess the summer has begun

The children are shouting
And arguing who has won
The boys are always showing off
I guess the summer has begun

I climb the monkey bars
Swinging from one to one
I eventually get to the end
I guess the summer is nearly done

I'm getting very cold
And getting really wet
I will miss this summer
I will never forget.

Jack Allison (10)
Our Lady of the Annunciation School, Glasgow

In The Forest

The crunching of the forest leaves
The smell of the ravenous wolves
The rustling of the trees' leaves
The cold breeze of the wind in the air

I see the animals running away
A red rose dying at my side
The horrible smell of burning wood
The thumping of a rabbit in its rabbit hole

The scales of a snake's body
I smell animals' droppings
The snapping of an oak tree's bark
The spikes of a thorn bush.

Antony Mellon (9)
Our Lady of the Annunciation School, Glasgow

In The Town

My reflection in the window
The clothes of the people
The display in the shops
The large shadows of the towering buildings

The buzzing of the voices
The thudding of my boots
The pitter-patter of the rain
The wailing of some babies

The leaking petrol from a car
Fish and chips from the shop
The smell of pollution
My mum's new perfume

My many shopping bags
The bumpy surface of the wall
My laces as I tie them
My bottle of juice

I'm very wet
As hot as an oven
My socks are soaking wet
I want to go home.

Anna Kennedy (9)
Our Lady of the Annunciation School, Glasgow

At A Football game

When I was at a football game
I saw the ball go in the back of the net
Over 50,000 fans jumping up and down

The fans swearing at each other
While others are singing songs with their friends
And one of the players arguing with the referee

The people making Bovril and pizza
For the customers.

Ryan Gallagher (10)
Our Lady of the Annunciation School, Glasgow

In The Town

People with shopping
The raindrops dropping
The shop doors open and close
My reflection from the shop windows

The engines on the cars roaring
The raindrops pouring
Some people asleep and snoring
Kids saying, 'Shopping is boring!'

The cars' smoke in the air
All the people's food to share
All the fit people eating pears

I look through the shop window
To see what is through them
The fake flower's long stem

The cold wind against my face
My speed picks up by the pace.

Steven Clark (9)
Our Lady of the Annunciation School, Glasgow

In World War II

I see German men falling, with blood coming from their heads.
I see American men flying from the German trenches.

I hear men screaming as they die on the ground.
I hear British tanks firing bombs at the German spy towers.

I smell the gas from the gas bombs.
I smell the polluted air.

I touch the steering wheel of the camouflaged trunk.
I touch the roughness of the ground as I fall.

I feel very afraid at night when I could be attacked at any time.
I feel I am risking my life, but for my country.

Mark Airlie (10)
Our Lady of the Annunciation School, Glasgow

At The Seaside

The waves racing into the shore.
The clouds moving across the sky.
The whirling of the water.
The feathers of the ducks.

The squawking of the seagulls.
The laughter of children.
The roaring of the engines of a speedboat.

The fresh sea air.
The fish in the sea.
The wet paint off the boats.

The smooth sand.
The bumpy walkway.
The crab's rough skin.
The handle of a spade.

The wind rushing through my hair.
Cold as the sea's water.
The scales of a starfish.
The clear soft body of a jellyfish.

Melissa McFarlane (10)
Our Lady of the Annunciation School, Glasgow

At The Football

The scoring of the players as the ball hits the net
The bright red flag of the home team and the dark green of the other

The cheering of the fans as they score
But as the other team score, they start to curse

The pies and pizzas from the shop
The beer I think it is lager, yes it is

The steel bars as I come down to my seat
The flag of pride as it goes over me

The wind as it hits my face
Cold, ten minutes to go as it is 3-1 to my team.

Adam Cavanagh (10)
Our Lady of the Annunciation School, Glasgow

In The Forest

The trees swaying around in the breeze
The birds hunting for food
The litter on the smooth town
The spiders making their sticky webs

The buzzing of the bees
The noise of the crickets
The rustling of the leaves
The rattling of the rattlesnake

The sweet honey in the beehive
The pollen on the daffodils
The feathers on the ground
The fleas on the bunnies

The smooth bark of the trees
The roughness of the ground
The fleece of a sheep
The face of my children afraid of the forest

The air in my face
As blind as a bat
As lonely as a tramp
As life will never change.

Paddy Campbell (9)
Our Lady of the Annunciation School, Glasgow

Glasgow

Every day in Glasgow people rush about going to work and school
Grampa reads his newspaper and Granny knits with her wool
People caught in traffic jams, huge lines of cars
Children going to the corner shop and buying chocolate bars
The clockwork orange underground
It makes a very loud sound
At the end of the day, everyone comes home for tea
I wonder what Mummy's made for me?
It's night-time, people have gone to bed
They'll need energy for the busy day ahead.

Sean Coyle (8)
Our Lady of the Annunciation School, Glasgow

At The Football Game

A midfielder taking a free-kick
The goalkeeper making a reflex save
A striker taking kick-off
The fans doing a Mexican wave

The sound of the ball being headed
The referee shouting as he pulls out the yellow
The ball being smacked up in the air
The bad tackle is made and the ref starts to bellow

The mince pies people are eating
The smell of the fresh grass in the stadium
The children eating toffee
The adults drinking coffee

I put on my coat when I get cold
I get bored of watching the game and touch the floor
I lean against my dad when I get sleepy
Twenty minutes to go and it starts to pour

I am very cold sitting for so long
I am very tired of watching the game
My socks are so wet, they are going to pong
I think my team are lucky winning 2-0.

Michael Dunne (9)
Our Lady of the Annunciation School, Glasgow

In The Park

My reflection in the pond
My shadow generating onto the ground
The greenhouse at the top of the hill
The sun shining in the can I have found

The tennis racket as it hits the ball
The wind as it passes by my ear
The children laugh as they go round the tree
The crowd watching the boats go past as they start to cheer

The pollen of the daffodils
The lovely fresh air
My dirty hands as I fall on the grass
The candyfloss from the fair

The water swirling between my fingers
My dad's hand as it reaches for my shoulder
The rough bark from the tree
The wind as it starts to get colder

As dumb as a post
A fish in the cold sea
As cold as metal
But I'm glad that it's just me.

James Gallacher (10)
Our Lady of the Annunciation School, Glasgow

A Football Match

A penalty being taken
It goes in
It was so good
And the other team were in a bad mood

The crowd roar
As some of them score
And they wanted more
As the other team were about to score

The hotdogs burning
The steam from the kitchen
The hotness of pies
The steamy oven

The railing to see
The ref gave me a key
And I gave him the ball

Very happy because his team won
For my best player to score.

Owen Sweeney (9)
Our Lady of the Annunciation School, Glasgow

Flying Pigs

Flying pigs come out at night,
As they don't like broad daylight,
Looking for some mice to eat,
Instead of eating farmers' wheat.

Sleeping in the barn all day,
Before coming out to play,
Some say they run, others say they jump,
One might even come down with a bump!

If you see a flying pig
You will be very lucky,
Sometimes when they come home at night
They are very mucky.

Patrick Hughes (8)
Our Lady of the Annunciation School, Glasgow

Seasons

In spring the birds come out singing
And the lambs start to walk, gallop and play
We have picnics out in the garden
Saying, 'What a lovely day'

In summer we go to the beach
Swimming and splashing about
We have ice cream and build sandcastles
The seagulls fly over us looking for some food

In autumn the leaves on the trees fall down
It gets colder each day
All the animals start to hibernate
Not many children go out to play
We have Hallowe'en parties in our houses

In winter, snow starts to cover the ground
Like a white carpet
Santa comes down people's chimneys
We decorate our Christmas trees
And get lots of presents.

Molly McGovern (8)
Our Lady of the Annunciation School, Glasgow

Summertime

S unny beaches, fun in the sun
U nder the umbrella eating ice creams
M unching sandwiches down by the sea
M aking huge sandcastles with buckets and spades
E veryone is having great fun
R oaring with laughter at the Punch and Judy show
T all lighthouses flashing away
 I n the sea jumping over waves
M illions of grains of sand running through my fingers
E veryone had a brilliant time.

Paul Grindlay (9)
Our Lady of the Annunciation School, Glasgow

Sun

In the morning the sun is coming up
The birds in the trees start to sing
And straight away I get up
I look out my window and I see something

I see the sun in the big blue sky
I run downstairs and outside I go
Down on the thick grass I do lie
The sun is moving very slow

Later in the afternoon the sun begins to fade
I go indoors where I can play
Where Mum has the table laid
It is nearly the end of the day

Now it's night, the sun has gone
I have some dinner and rest my head
The sun will appear at dawn
I go upstairs and into bed.

Charlotte Jack (9)
Our Lady of the Annunciation School, Glasgow

Rainforest Surprises

As I walk through very calm,
Peacefully eating a roll of ham,
The water from the waterfall is crystal-clear,
In the rainforest there is nothing to fear.
Sticks and stones on the forest floor,
I wish I could see much more,
Cute animals running around,
Not even making a sound.
I see pretty exotic flowers,
The rain here is like little showers.
I hear birds singing,
Instead of my phone ringing.
So start saving the rainforest today,
Then, it could pay you back some other day.

Laura Quinn (11)
Our Lady of the Annunciation School, Glasgow

Seasons

In spring when blossoms come out
The children go out to play
They don't care if they have sun or not
They just try to have a good day

In summer when school time ends
The children go on holiday
They run about and scream and shout
All day long they're out to play

In autumn when the leaves begin to fall
The children can't wait for Hallowe'en
They like to dress up
Especially for the sweets

In winter when it starts to snow
The children run about, faces have a rosy glow
They can't wait till Christmas comes
Santa's on his way.

Mairi Benham (9)
Our Lady of the Annunciation School, Glasgow

Battlefield

On the battlefield many bullets fly
Many men die
Hear the tanks rumble
See the buildings crumble

See the planes fly
Like birds in the sky
When these planes attack
There is no turning back

Men running fast
To escape the guns' blast
There is chaos all around
They hate that deafening sound.

I'm glad I wasn't there!

Scott Donachy (10)
Our Lady of the Annunciation School, Glasgow

The Moon

Sometimes when the sky is clear,
I can see the moon appear
And because it is so big and bright,
It sets the whole night sky alight.

When my supper is all done
And in its bed sleeps the sun,
The moon will rise up with its light
And whisper to me, *sleep tight!*

So when I cannot get to sleep,
Instead of starting to count sheep,
I gaze out my window at the moon
And I know I will go to sleep soon.

So the moon is good in many ways,
Out of my window I do gaze,
At the absolutely delightful moon,
As sunshine awaits to come up soon.

Hannah Ruddy (9)
Our Lady of the Annunciation School, Glasgow

At The Seaside

I see
The sparkling water as it goes over the rocks
A scuttling crab as it seeks some shade
The rolling clouds making shapes and shadows

I hear
Squirting sun cream bottles as people put it on
The laughing children dancing in the sun
Seagulls crying and diving in the sea

I smell
Tangy seawater as it's washed on the shore
The fishy food from a nearby café
Chips from a packet not far away.

Andrew Brown (9)
Our Lady of the Annunciation School, Glasgow

At The Seaside

The beautiful shells sitting by my feet
The choppy waves, bumping up and down
The seagulls flying above my head
The seals swimming through the clear blue water

Waves crashing off the rocks
The seagulls squawking
The children paddling in the water

The salty sea air
The crabs in the seafood restaurant
The sweat of the donkeys carrying people along
The salty seaweed around my feet

The crisp ice cream cone
The smooth seaweed
The golden sand
The cold seawater

The ice cream touching my tongue
The wind against my face
I want to read my book on the lounger
And have some freshly squeezed orange
Juice to drink.

Meghan Hughes (9)
Our Lady of the Annunciation School, Glasgow

Will

Will Harry Potter cast a spell
on the big ringing bell?

Will Shakespeare write another play
and be the hero of the day?

Will Leonardo become a stitcher
or will he paint another picture?

Will Sunny Baudelaire start to talk
or will she begin to walk?

David Conkie (8)
Our Lady of the Annunciation School, Glasgow

Battlefield

The screaming, shouting, yelling in pain,
Apart from deaths,
What will this gain?

I see blood from soldiers,
Too many deaths.
I see nurses helping,
Putting others to rest.

I think of empty hearts that surround me,
I think of the shock their families would endure
If they could see what I see . . .
The meaning of war.

I feel the hard ground under my feet,
This is where all enemies meet,
I feel all the hearts that have no meaning,
All the others beating and pleading . . .

This is a battlefield.

Rachel Sharp (10)
Our Lady of the Annunciation School, Glasgow

Summer

Summertime is so much fun
Ice cream for everyone
We've all come down to play
It's a good day at the bay
Munching away at my bun
In the warmth of the sun
Then we went into the sea
Big waves splashing over me
Later, when we walked away
We said, 'What fun we had today.'

Stuart McGibbon (9)
Our Lady of the Annunciation School, Glasgow

Blitzed London

'Tis 1942 the year of the London blitz
The morning has awoken from her dreadful sleep
Every day is the same
The smell of rubble, dust and fumes, poisons our great city

These are tough times
Where people are always rushing to receive their rations
Everywhere bomb shelters can be seen
Thousands of people running in fear of their lives

Now the terrifying night is upon us
The warning sirens like the Devil's cry are ringing out like demons
As quick as a flash everyone is out of the door looking up
The bombers, how their hearts must be as cold as ice

In the bomb shelter, above us the deadly metal rains down
                                        from the sky
Then like an evil cry, a screeching bomb lands next to your shelter
Suddenly your heart stops, your senses stop and life itself
                                        seems to end
All the while, people think the world has ended.

John Carson (11)
Our Lady of the Annunciation School, Glasgow

At The Beach

I can hear waves as they rise up onto the shore.
I can see people lying under parasols, enjoying the sun.
I can smell the salt in the air.
I can feel the soft sand run through my fingers.
I feel great!

Jennifer Marley (9)
Our Lady of the Annunciation School, Glasgow

The Woods

The woods are dark and exciting,
New memories entering my heart.

I see green dappled light shining through the canopy
A flick of a bird's wing, the fluttering of a butterfly,
Crawling, scuttling, scampering beasts in the undergrowth,
Dragon-like trees bending towards us in the musty dusk.

The woods are dark and exciting,
New memories entering my heart.

I hear creaking ropes and screaming excitement
Of the rope-swing fun,
Squelching, oozing mud like lava beside the stream
That flows like silver,
Cracking branches and scrunched leaves,
Clues given away during hide-and-seek.

The woods are dark and exciting,
New memories entering my heart.

I smell rotting fruits, attracting ants and bees,
Sneezing fits after kicking up leaves,
Delightful explosions of colour sending out trails of perfume.

The woods are dark and exciting,
New memories entering my heart.

Kathryn Marley (10)
Our Lady of the Annunciation School, Glasgow

Senses Of The Rainforest

There's loads of life in the rainforest.

You see the bright colourful plants
and beside them the scurrying killer ants.
You see the busy branches of the canopy,
the forest floor teeming with insects.

There's loads of life in the rainforest.

You hear the loud panthers roaring
while the screeching fruit-bat's soaring.
You hear the howling monkeys swinging
over the small wild boar's snorting.

There's loads of life in the rainforest.

You smell the tropical flowers like scented candles,
under the trees that are skyscrapers,
are the rotting leaves that are being devoured.

There's loads of life in the rainforest.

You feel so hot trekking through the forest
that you feel annoyed.
I feel sad that the rainforest is
being destroyed.

There's loads of life in the rainforest.

Bernadette Campbell (11)
Our Lady of the Annunciation School, Glasgow

Working Together!

If we all work together,
We'll get what we want;
Bigotry binned
And tolerance brought out.

Together we can fight it,
We've just got to be kind,
Helping and loving,
Let's put sectarianism behind.

Then we can rejoice,
Sit down and be safe,
Come out, work together
And then we can shout,

'The bigots are binned,
Racism's in the past,
Our children are safe,
Finally, at long last!'

Together united,
Forever it should stay,
It's not to happen soon,
It will happen today!

Sarah Airlie (12)
Our Lady of the Annunciation School, Glasgow

Monkeys

M onkeys like bananas
O ut and about looking for food
N oisy, always laughing all day
K icking and swinging from tree to tree
E ating like mad again
Y elling to each other
S ound asleep now.

Lauren McAreavey (8)
Our Lady of the Annunciation School, Glasgow

The Tolerant Clan

Tolerance is good
Intolerance is bad
Tolerant, tolerant, you just have to be tolerant
Don't be bad, just be good
And follow the tolerant *clan!*

If you want to be bad,
Try a new start,
Try a *shot* at the clan.

Switch from bad to good,
Don't switch from good to bad,
Now it's getting bigger,
Come along to the clan *party*,
Don't be an intolerant boy or girl,
Ha ha, we are nearly finished
But remember,
Do not follow the intolerant gang!

Ben Moran (11)
Our Lady of the Annunciation School, Glasgow

Tolerance

T ogether, united, how we should stay.
O thers matter, that's what we say.
L iving in harmony, that's how it should be.
E verybody's equal, that's the key!
R acism is pointless, racism is bad.
A lthough different skin, there's no need to feel sad.
N o one should worry about who they are.
C olours, teams, religions, will only leave a scar.
E veryone is different but everyone's the same.
  So let's stop all this fighting
  It's driving us insane!

Gemma West (11)
Our Lady of the Annunciation School, Glasgow

In The Town

The little babies running round the shop
Shopkeepers trying to sell their goods
People eating their lunch in the café
Friends looking for birthday cards

Children laughing
Cars beeping at one another
The splashing of the fountain
The barking of some dogs

The hot chocolate from outside the coffee shop
Chicken burgers
The petrol from the cars' engines
The beautiful fresh flowers

The cold bottle of water
The warm chips on a plate
The soft lavender on the bar of soap

The cooling of the wind on my cheeks
The freshness of the fresh air
My hair waving about in the breeze.

Lucy Middleton (10)
Our Lady of the Annunciation School, Glasgow

Holidays

I can see kids running to the sea and people getting cold drinks.
I feel my bare feet in the sand, burning from the heat of the sun.
I hear children laughing while the waves go by and adults
saying, 'This is the life!'
I smell the sweetness of chocolate ice cream and the
bitterness of the seaweed.
I feel happy.

Olivia Gough (9)
Our Lady of the Annunciation School, Glasgow

In The Town

My reflection in a shop window
Colourful car whizzing past
Rubbish dumped on the ground
Bright flowers in a pot

Children shouting
Birds chirping
The whistling of the wind
The singing of the happy crowd

Scent of the flowers as I pass a flower stall
Petrol from the cars
Fish and chips
People's perfume when they walk past

The rough pavement hits against my heel
A cold bottle of water out of a café
The smooth shop window pane
The smooth bark of a tree

The cold wind whooshing past me
The sun shining on me
My ice-lolly melting on my hand.

Eve Gordon (10)
Our Lady of the Annunciation School, Glasgow

Snakes

S nakes slither in the long green grass
N ever making a sound
A lways trying to stay hidden
K nowing when something is going to appear
E yes looking all about
S uddenly a rabbit comes out . . . *gulp!*

Balal Saleemi (9)
Our Lady of the Annunciation School, Glasgow

In The Forest

The coloured feathers of a duck
The enormous oak tree
A pack of wolves in their den
Rabbits in a rabbit hole beside a thorn bush

I hear the slithering of a grass snake through the grass
The splashing of the waterfall
The rattle of a rattlesnake
The rustling of leaves

The smell of animals' droppings
Fresh mud and rosebuds
The smell of a red rose
The smell of berries on the rosebush

The crunchy leaves
The rough bark on the oak tree
The spikes on the thorn bush
The scales on the grass snake.

Kamil Demiroz (9)
Our Lady of the Annunciation School, Glasgow

In The Park

My reflection in the pond
The long green grass
The rough concrete that makes the path
The bush full of berries

The rustling of the leaves
The twittering of the birds
The splashing of the pond
The wind blowing

The sweet honey of the bees
The newly-cut grass
The weeds in the middle of the pond
The fresh mud.

James Forrester (9)
Our Lady of the Annunciation School, Glasgow

In The Park

Children going down the slide
My reflection in the pond
Birds high in the air
The green grass under my feet

The boys and girls screaming
Birds singing
The swing squeaking as it goes up and down
The splashing of the fountain

The yellow dandelions
The fresh air
The squishy mud

The monkey bars
The cold metal bar of the swing

Happy as a bird
Excited forever.

Megan Darroch (9)
Our Lady of the Annunciation School, Glasgow

At The Seaside

Children making sandcastles
Children splashing in the sea
The seagulls flying high in the air

The sand brushing down the shore
People screaming at the cold water

The fresh air
The cold ice cream

The salty water
The bumpy shells

Happy as ever
Good as the birds.

Grace Symes (9)
Our Lady of the Annunciation School, Glasgow

In The Town

Cars rushing along the street
People waiting for buses
The rain reflecting off streetlights

Rumbling of the cars' engines
The beeping of horns
The rattling of the trains

The pollution gases
The smoke of cars' exhausts
The food of a restaurant

The old windows of an old taxi
The cold metal bars of a motorbike
The stray black cat

The coldness of an old alley
The frustration of the children
The happiness of adults watching TV.

Daniel Milgrew (9)
Our Lady of the Annunciation School, Glasgow

Linn Park

Linn Park is a beautiful sight
Even when it is cold at night
When it is sunny and warm at day
Children always laugh and play

The colourful park is full of squirrels and foxes
Lots of open spaces with horses in their boxes
The clear water flowing with gentle ease
The waterfall's spray is spread in the breeze

When I go there for a nightly walk
I feel relaxed, happy and free to talk
Running ahead to find trees to climb
It gives me a chance to forget about time.

Linn Park is a beautiful sight.

Paul McMahon (10)
Our Lady of the Annunciation School, Glasgow

The Blitz

All is quiet in London,
The deafening silence rules over us.

Then the dreadful siren goes off,
People scream and shout,
They run to their shelters,
Safe at last.
Then the thundering bombs fell like coconuts
Destroying everything they touch.
Buildings are demolished one by one,
The blinding lights flash,
Homes are destroyed.
The German planes fly like angels of death,
The bombs strike like lightning,
The noise stops and the siren goes off again.

All is quiet in London
The deafening silence rules over us.

Luke Robertson (11)
Our Lady of the Annunciation School, Glasgow

My Street

Next door neighbours, Bob and Jessy
Hardly see them
They're like Nessy
Big long street
With a school at the top
Has a big strenuous hill
With a steep sheer drop
Big tall houses
Ancient, old or modern, new
Small fences hiding the gardens
Where daisies grow
But even though I feel settled in
Part of me feels there's time to spare.

Kerry Connolly (11)
Our Lady of the Annunciation School, Glasgow

Precious Rainforests

Rainforests are precious
To all mankind,
Rainforests keep secrets
For us to find.

Rainforests are precious
To all mankind,
The crisp leaves crumple
From herb giving trees.

Rainforests are precious
To all mankind,
Feeling all different
Textures of tree bark.

Rainforests are precious
To all mankind,
Now go and find
Its many precious secrets.

Martin McLaughlin (10)
Our Lady of the Annunciation School, Glasgow

Glasgow

Glasgow is the best
Full of parks, shops and buildings
Many sights to see

Parks like Linn Park are a sight
Especially at night
Glasgow is known for beautiful parks

You can always hear the cars and people
In the city centre, full of shops
People are in and out as quick as a flash

Glasgow is the best
It always beats the rest.

Steven Benham (10)
Our Lady of the Annunciation School, Glasgow

Forest Floor

On the forest floor
A fight has begun
Vipers and anacondas
Battle for the title of
The best snake in the forest

In the understory
A black widow's creeping
Up towards the sun

In the canopy
The howler monkey calls
To his far-off mate
But she is in a fight
Is it too late?

In the emergent layer
The eagle lands near her young
With field mice in her mouth.

Jordan Devine (10)
Our Lady of the Annunciation School, Glasgow

Save The Rainforest

Animals could keep secrets
When day is dawning
With animals shouting
Squirrels jumping from branch to branch
While birds prey on small animals
People hunt birds for a sport
Others hunt panthers for a fur coat
Stop them chopping down trees
Or one day at dusk
All the trees that are as green as an apple
Will not be there because they have been destroyed
And all animals in the rainforest will be gone
With no homes or food, they'll all die.

Barry Morgan (10)
Our Lady of the Annunciation School, Glasgow

Wonders Of The Rainforest

Howling monkeys, hissing snakes
Screeching monkeys all around the place
How does this make you feel?
Quiet forest, peaceful forest
Everywhere is a lovely forest
What does this make you feel?
Seeing monkeys swinging from tree to tree
Hearing monkeys howling at sunset
Smelling tropical fruit
How does this make you feel?
The later it gets, the wind is as cool as a breeze
Later, the sun goes down
Animals start to settle into their homes
As the hours go by
The animals are settled in

So keep the forest.

Kelsey Lipton (10)
Our Lady of the Annunciation School, Glasgow

In The Town

My reflection on the wide bright window
As all the people queue up to watch the latest film

The drumming of the rain on the tall streetlight
The stray fierce cat purring
The gurgle of the water flowing down the drain

The horrible gas pollution from the diesel fumes
The strong scent of the coffee beans

The smooth furry coat in a shop
The cold silvery banister as I descend.

Aidan McKendrick (9)
Our Lady of the Annunciation School, Glasgow

Think About The Rainforest

Forest floor with mud and insects,
Understory quite the same.
Canopy brings some light in but,
Emergent layer has it all,
Think about the trees, the trees, the trees,
Help us save the rainforest!

The plants are full of medicine,
Which could easily save lives.
The plants can also provide homes for animals,
Who are passing through.
Think about the plants, the plants, the plants,
Help us save the rainforest!

Some animals are rare and the rainforest
Is where you will find them.
So don't destroy animals' homes,
Think about them when you leave the light on,
Think about the animals, the animals, the animals,
Help us save the rainforest.

Evlyn Russell (10)
Our Lady of the Annunciation School, Glasgow

Seasons

S pring is a time when everything is growing,
E verywhere new life appears,
A nimals are born,
S ummer is when we can play outside,
O n sunny days,
N o one wants it to end,
S easons make a changing year.

Liam Macpherson (9)
Our Lady of the Annunciation School, Glasgow

My Best Friends

My best friends are Bernie, Janet,
Sophie, Gamma, Durdane and Tammi.
They all play with me.
We like to chatter
And play games together
And sometimes they come
To my house for a party.

Maram Elfleet (11)
Richmond Park School, Glasgow

Bernie Rap

She is my best friend
We never fight
We will be best friends
Forever and ever
She went to nursery with me
Sometimes she comes home for tea
I care about her a lot.

Jodie Taylor (11)
Richmond Park School, Glasgow

My Best Friends

My best friends are Sean, Dean, David and Kyle
We all love to smile
We talk whilst we walk
We get a good laugh in the baths
Due to Dean being very daft
We then go to the park until it's dark
Then we all head home together.

William Marshall (10)
Richmond Park School, Glasgow

My Granny

G reat, graceful and gorgeous
R easonable and responsible
A ctive when you were young
N ever sad
N ever nagging at my dad
Y ou were my granny and now I'm sad.

Dean Burrell (11)
Richmond Park School, Glasgow

The Haunted House

In the hall is
A broken rocking chair
Creaky floorboards
Rusty pots and pans
A death trap
And the only sounds
Are footsteps

In the dungeon are
Skeletons
Bats
Spiders
Ripped clothes
And the only sound is
Tapping

In the garden are
Moving eyes
Dead spiders
Broken skulls
Rats' tails
And the only sound is
Howling.

Josh Moody (8)
Rimbleton Primary School, Glenrothes

The Haunted House

In the kitchen are
Death traps beside the door
Creaky floorboards, rusty pots and pans
Old chairs that snap when you sit on them
And the only sound is
Tapping on the window

In the hall are
Old and rotting bananas and oranges
Broken, dusty toys, burnt letters on the table
And a rickety old staircase
And the only sound is
Footsteps

In the dungeon are
Old, ripped and burnt clothes
Bats and dead spiders
Skeletons everywhere
And the only sound is
Bats flying.

Amy McKillop (9)
Rimbleton Primary School, Glenrothes

The Haunted House

In the attic
A doll with one leg
A rotten apple, a big cobweb
And ripped ribbons
And the only sound is
Clicking

In the kitchen is
A rotten lemon
A sink full of bones and blood
Rusty pots and pans
And the only sound is
Squeaky floorboards.

Graham McSeveney (8)
Rimbleton Primary School, Glenrothes

The Haunted House

In the hall are
Creaky floorboards
And when you walk through
It is very spooky
There are broken windows
Also big spiders and the
Only sound is tapping on the walls

In the kitchen are
Rusty pots and cobwebs
And there is water dripping
Doors are squeaking
Branches rustling
And the only sounds are
Footsteps

In the music room are
Old chairs
And burnt letters
And also lots of moving eyes
And bats on the roof
And the only sound is the
Organ playing

In the bathroom are
Dead spiders on the floor
And cobwebs on the ceiling
Death traps in the bath
Handprints of blood on the wall
And the only sound is the
Branches rustling against the windows.

Liam McKinney (8)
Rimbleton Primary School, Glenrothes

The Haunted House

In the kitchen are
Bats flying, dead spiders
Death traps and creaky floorboards
And the only sound is
Howling

In the garden are
Bats flying, spiders on the coffins
Skulls falling from trees and old bodies
And the only sounds are
Bats squealing

In the music room is a
Singing piano covered in spiders
A death trap and burnt letters
And the only sound is
The floor squeaking

In the attic is a
Doll with one leg, a rotten apple
An old chair and a dusty tin trunk
And the only sound is
The wind whistling.

Jamie Farmer (8)
Rimbleton Primary School, Glenrothes

A Poem Of Feelings

When I am amused, I feel as purple as the dancing flowers.
When I feel happy, I feel as blue as the summer sparkling ocean.
When I am hurt, I feel as orange as the sunset at night.
When I feel unhappy, I feel as silvery as the glowing stars.
When I feel scared, I feel as yellow as the shining sun.
When I am nervous, I feel as white as a plain piece of paper.
When I feel angry, I feel as black as a blackboard.
When I am furious, I feel as red as boiling hot lava.

Katie Walker (8)
Rimbleton Primary School, Glenrothes

The Haunted House

In the kitchen is
A skull in the oven
A blood stew
A bone getting fried
A cup of blood
And the only sound is
Footsteps

In the bathroom is
A dead body
A vampire in the bath
A spider in the toilet
A big cobweb in the sink
And the only sound is
Water dripping

In the attic is
A box of heads
A toy box with dead animals in it
A skeleton on the roof
A ghost in the tissue box
And the only sounds are
Vampires laughing.

Connor Currie (9)
Rimbleton Primary School, Glenrothes

A Poem Of Feelings

When I feel surprised, I feel as blue as the blowing ocean.
When I feel happy, I feel as silvery as the sparkling stars.
When I feel furious, I feel as red as the flowing lava.
When I feel selfish, I feel as silvery as the glowing moon.
When I feel sad, I feel as white as a blowing daisy.
When I feel brave, I feel as black as the blackboard.
When I feel jealous, I feel as green as the swishy grass.
When I feel hurt, I feel as grey as the cloudy sky.

Yasmine Petrie (8)
Rimbleton Primary School, Glenrothes

The Haunted House

In the bedroom there are
Ripped clothes
Moving eyes
Squeaky doors
Skeletons
And the only sounds are
Bats flying.

In the kitchen there are
Rusty pots and pans
Water dripping
Old chairs
Doors knocking
And the only sounds are
Windows smashing.

In the dining room there are
Light bulbs flashing
Creaking floorboards
Dead spiders
Two pianos covered in cobwebs
And the only sound is
Thunder and lightning.

Deni Latimer (8)
Rimbleton Primary School, Glenrothes

My Feelings Poem

When I feel happy, I feel as yellow as a dancing daffodil.
When I feel brave, I feel as black as the blackboard.
When I feel angry, I feel as red as the boiling lava.
When I feel confused, I feel as white as the page on my workbook.
When I feel adventurous, I feel as golden as a pot of glittering gold.
When I feel anxious, I feel as green as the long grass.
When I am selfish, I feel as grey as the floor.
When I am honest, I feel as orange as the sunrise.

Jordan Farrell (9)
Rimbleton Primary School, Glenrothes

Through The Door

(Inspired by 'Go and Open the Door' by Miroslav Holub)

Go and open the door
Perhaps you'll see
A baby crying or
Cars on the road
Or maybe you'll see
A five-headed alien or
People walking upside-down
But don't be afraid
Go and open the door

Go and open the door
Perhaps you'll see
People playing or
Alfie and Olivia smiling back at you
Or maybe you'll see
A talking cat or
A flying car
But don't be afraid
Go and open the door.

Samantha Riddell (8)
Rimbleton Primary School, Glenrothes

My Poem Of Feelings

When I feel happy, I feel as yellow as the dancing flowers.
When I feel nervous, I feel as silvery as the stars in the sky.
When I feel confused, I feel as clear as the sky.
When I feel angry, I feel as red as the flowing lava.
When I feel brave, I feel as black as the blackboard.
When I feel excited, I feel as green as the grass.
When I feel scared, I feel as peachy as a ghost on my back.
When I feel sad, I feel as orange as the beans dancing in the tin.

Connor Herd (9)
Rimbleton Primary School, Glenrothes

Through The Door

(Inspired by 'Go and Open the Door' by Miroslav Holub)

Go and open the door
Perhaps you will see
A fish in the sea
And a shell on the beach
Or maybe you will see
A dragon with a flying fish for tea
Or more dragons with more flying fish for tea
But don't be afraid
Go and open the door.

Go and open the door
Perhaps you will see
A garden full of flowers
Tons of toys in my bed
Or maybe you will see
A dog playing chess
Or a cat in a hat
But don't be afraid
Go and open the door.

Amy Kirkum (9)
Rimbleton Primary School, Glenrothes

The Feelings Poem

When I am feeling happy, I feel as yellow as the dancing sun.
When I am feeling furious, I feel as red as the hot flowing lava.
When I am feeling sad, I feel as blue as the wavy sea.
When I am feeling adventurous, I feel as green as the swishy grass.
When I am feeling excited, I feel as silvery as the sparkling stars.
When I am feeling nervous, I feel as grey as the foggy sky.
When I am feeling moody, I feel as brown as the rough trees.
When I am feeling brave, I feel as black as the starry night.

Sarah-Jane Brand (9)
Rimbleton Primary School, Glenrothes

Through The Door

(Inspired by 'Go and Open the Door' by Miroslav Holub)

Go and open the door
Perhaps you'll see
A baby crying
People going to the shops
Or maybe you'll see
A dog with eight legs
An elephant coming for tea
But don't be afraid
Go and open the door.

Go and open the door
Perhaps you'll see
People playing
Someone taking their dog for a walk
Or maybe you'll see
A cat with two heads
A tree with a face
But don't be afraid
Go and open the door.

Kirsty Howard (8)
Rimbleton Primary School, Glenrothes

My Poem Of Feelings

When I feel furious, I feel as red as the boiling hot lava.
When I feel happy, I feel as yellow as the dancing daffodils.
When I am honest, I feel as silvery as the shining moon.
When I feel brave, I feel as black as the starry night.
When I feel adventurous, I feel as golden as a pot of sparkling gold.
When I feel jealous, I feel as brown as a big tree.
When I feel hurt, I feel as white as a football.
When I feel excited, I feel as peachy as a flowerpot.

Katie Jenkins (8)
Rimbleton Primary School, Glenrothes

The Haunted House

In the hall is
A booby-trapped door
Creaking floorboards
A big spooky cobweb
A vampire's tooth
And the only sounds are
Footsteps in the distance.

In the garden are
Some gravestones
A rusty bike
Long wavy grass
A big long hedge
And the only sounds are
Tall trees blowing.

Grant Donaldson (9)
Rimbleton Primary School, Glenrothes

The Haunted House

In the hall are
Spiders webs
Dusty and broken toys
Spilled and rotten apples
Broken lights
And the only sound is
Water dripping

In the dining room is
A pile of rat's food
Dead spiders all over the floor
Broken chairs
A fuzzy television
And the only sound is
Footsteps tapping.

Troi Scott (9)
Rimbleton Primary School, Glenrothes

The Haunted House

In the hallway is
An old trunk, dusty bones
An old bicycle chain
A rusty shoe buckle
And the only sound is
A leaking pipe

In the bedroom is an
Old bed
It has a snake
A snail and a frog's leg
And the only sound is
Rustling

In the cellar is
An old chair
Covered with mice and rats
Hopping and dancing about
And the only sound is
Scratching.

Rona Hamilton (8)
Rimbleton Primary School, Glenrothes

The Haunted House

In the spooky kitchen
Are broken pots and pans
Rusty plates in the cupboard
The cooker burning away
And the only sounds are
People laughing.

In the bedroom there
Are broken toys and ripped clothes
An old piano covered in cobwebs
And moving eyes
And the only sounds are
Creaking footsteps.

Jade Harper (8)
Rimbleton Primary School, Glenrothes

Through The Door

(Inspired by 'Go and Open the Door' by Miroslav Holub)

Go and open the door
Perhaps you'll see
Children going to school or
Mums pushing prams
Or maybe you'll see
Dogs playing cards or
Aliens attacking Earth
But don't be afraid
Go and open the door.

Go and open the door
Perhaps you'll see
Cars on the road or
Your mum doing the gardening
Or maybe you'll see
A dragon coming for tea or a
Dog doing the shopping
But don't be afraid
Go and open the door.

Barry Kerr (8)
Rimbleton Primary School, Glenrothes

A Poem Of Feelings

When I feel happy, I feel as yellow as the bright sun.
When I am angry, I feel as red as the fiery hot lava.
When I am honest, I feel as violet as the dancing flowers.
When I feel excited, I feel as a blue as the big sky.
When I feel brave, I feel as green as the long grass.
When I am amused, I feel as pink as the cuddly teddy.
When I feel sad, I feel as grey as the pencil sharpener.
When I am scared, I feel as black as the night sky.

Megan Cameron (8)
Rimbleton Primary School, Glenrothes

My Poem Of Feelings

When I feel happy, I feel as green as the wavy grass.
When I feel angry, I feel as red as the hot lava.
When I feel jealous, I feel as yellow as the bright sun.
When I feel excited, I feel as silvery as the sparkling moon.
When I feel sad, I feel as black as the dark clouds.
When I feel scared, I feel as orange as my comfy bed.
When I feel nervous, I feel as brown as the rooftops.
When I feel curious, I feel as blue as the clear sky.

Aidan Kirkwood (8)
Rimbleton Primary School, Glenrothes

Shipwrecked

The drunken pirates with a bottle of run,
Shipwrecked on an island of danger.
They built a shelter and made a raft
But they just went back to the lagoon.
They sent a bottle with a note,
'Can you help us get a new boat'.
They found some treasure with lots of balloons,
They bought a boat and got off this harmful island.

Jordan Wright (11)
St Angela's Primary School, Glasgow

Trampolines

Every day when I come home from school,
I run to the back garden and it's very cool,
Right before my eyes is a giant trampoline,
I go on it every day because I'm the bouncing queen.
In five minutes I'm in the stars twirling and flipping,
Shooting past Mars,
But when I come bouncing back to Earth,
I'm puffing and panting, gasping for breath.

Chloé McNamee (12)
St Angela's Primary School, Glasgow

Beauty Pageant

Beautiful costumes, lovely gowns,
They wish for world peace but that goes unannounced.
Happiness is great, travelling is fine,
I feel great, pity, not allowed wine!
Getting ready,
Hair, make-up, consider it done,
Gosh, choosing clothes is such fun!
This experience is far greater than none,
A small breeze drifting through the stage,
It's like a dreamy daze.
The mistress is here, oh, I'm trembling with fear!
Announcing the queen is so near!
Being nervous is normal, I'm trying to look formal!
Happiness is great, tension is high,
To three girls we say goodbye!
No glaring faces, no foul play,
We all win anyway!

Courtney Hollis (11)
St Angela's Primary School, Glasgow

Hard Life In School

In my school, I'm really smart,
My favourite subject is art.
I am better than someone called Mark.
I drew a picture of a shark
When I was in Queen's park.
Now I am an artist
And part-time smartest.
Now I'm off to high school,
I hear they have a swimming pool.
The swimming instructor is a right fool!

Charlene Lang (11)
St Angela's Primary School, Glasgow

Jealousy

Why didn't you come out at the weekend with me?
Doesn't it matter? Because it matters to me
Why do you hang out with all your 'other friends'?
It was meant to be me and you until the end
Well, if things have changed, then why can't it be
That you play with the others and also with me?
Is it because they're cooler, with plenty of style
And to hang out with me, they'd rather run a mile?
Though we had our rough times, which were both lonely and sad,
I never thought it would be this bad.
If you offer to meet me, you're an hour or so late
And you say you were out with the rest of the your mates,
At the end of the road it's got to be . . .
You have to choose, them or me?

Gemma Bradley (11)
St Angela's Primary School, Glasgow

The Rainforest

The rainforest is big, the rainforest isn't bright,
The rainforest is swampy, the rainforest is just fine.

The monkeys give a cheeky laugh at the ground below.
To the animals on the forest floor
Who can't climb high or low.
As for the jaguars and tigers
They show their ferocious teeth to the monkeys
Telling them to stop and go!

The macaws fly freely above the trees,
Up into the crystal-clear, blue sky,
Flying together they look like a lovely,
Big, colourful rainbow standing out
So well in the big blue sky.

Humza Iqbal (12)
St Angela's Primary School, Glasgow

Teachers

Teachers drive you crazy!
And up the wall,
They always think they know it all.

They scream and shout
And make you doubt,
That you could ever get through this class,
They'd show you up in front of a crowd
And embarrass you clear and loud.

But just remember,
Teachers are there to help,
Not to *shout!*

Kathleen Shaw (11)
St Angela's Primary School, Glasgow

Drugs

Drugs are bad,
Drugs are sad,
Sometimes you're glad,
But they make you mad,
There's a risk
That you might
Break the disk,
But I have one
Thing to say,
Don't be the mug that
Takes the drug.

Peter Merrick (11)
St Angela's Primary School, Glasgow

On Board A Pirate Ship

When on board a pirate ship,
You will encounter ruthless pirates.
They stink, they smell, they shoot, they kill,
Would you enter the danger ship?
The pirates arrive, with big black eye patches,
Big round hooks,
Giant long peg legs
And silly old pig tails.
They're all vengeful, murderous, black-hearted, greedy men,
Why follow the Jolly Roger is you know it would
Put your life at stake?
Just enjoy your life and stay away from Jolly Roger.

Cuebong Wong (12)
St Angela's Primary School, Glasgow

My Dog, Mia

My dog, Mia was once a pup
In the night she would wake you up
My dog, Mia is no longer a pup
'Cause look at her now, she's all grown up
My dog, Mia is one year old
In dog years she is seven years old
My dog, Mia is no average dog
'Cause she is a sheepdog
But she doesn't work on a farm
She stays at home with me!

Shannon McGregor (11)
St Angela's Primary School, Glasgow

The Most Important

I'm your teacher
I taught you it all
I told you why you shouldn't fall
If you couldn't read or write
Where would you be?
So, the most important here, is me!

Who are you kidding?
Are you taking the mick?
Who makes you better
When you're feeling sick?
I'm a doctor
And always on call
So, I'm more important than you all!

But I'm your mother
Don't forget me
If it wasn't for your mother
Where would you be?
I washed your nappies
And washed your vest
So I'm the most important
And Mummy knows best

Just hold on, I've something to say
Let's all make a circle and all remember this
Who's the most important?
Everybody is!

Emma Hannah (11)
St Angela's Primary School, Glasgow

Television

I like watching TV, it's exciting
And delightful
I like watching TV, even though
It can be frightful
Soaps, cartoons and movies
They really are such fun
My favourite is The Simpsons
I've watched nearly every one
TV rots your brain so the adults say
But that's not what I read in
The papers yesterday
A clever man has said that it
Can be good for you
It can help your brain work faster
I wonder if that's true
You can learn things from TV
Not only from the news
But from educational programmes
And documentaries too
You can see around the world
How poor people live
And when some people watch this
It really does make them give
I like reading books, they can help me with my tests
But if you asked me honestly, I'd say TV is the best!

Sara Boussouara (11)
St Angela's Primary School, Glasgow

I'm Not Feeling Well

Blocked nose,
Loud sneezes,
Dead tired,
Feeling sick.

No appetite,
Paper hankies,
Doctor's visit,
Feeling sick.

Itchy rash,
Red spots,
Cough bottle,
But feeling better.

Bright eyes,
Tummy rumbling,
Ready for school,
Feeling fine.

James Jackson (8)
St Brigid's Primary School, Newmains

My Cold

Colds are sore throats,
Colds are runny noses,
Does anyone want my cold?

Colds aren't marvellous,
Colds are splendid,
Does anyone want my cold?

Colds are ghastly,
Colds are dreadful,
Doesn't anybody want my cold?

Aileen McKenna (8)
St Brigid's Primary School, Newmains

I'm Not Feeling Well

Runny nose,
Swollen eyes,
Throbbing head,
Feeling sick.

Itchy rash,
Red spots,
Dead tired,
Feeling sick.

No appetite,
Cough bottle,
Paper hankies,
But feeling better.

Eager to play,
Clear head,
Ready for school,
Feeling fine!

Declan Sinclair (8)
St Brigid's Primary School, Newmains

My Colds

Colds are sore throats,
Colds are high temperatures,
Does anyone want my cold?

Colds aren't nice,
Colds aren't good fun,
Does anyone want my cold?

Colds are dreadful,
Colds are awful,
Doesn't anyone want my cold?

Megan Stewart (8)
St Brigid's Primary School, Newmains

I'm Not Feeling Well

Heavy eyes,
Itchy rash,
Dead tired,
Feeling sick.

Chesty cough,
Loud sneezes,
Thumping head,
Feeling sick.

Paper hankies,
Cough bottle,
No appetite,
But feeling better.

Bright eyes,
Ready for school,
Medicine finished,
Feeling fine!

Kelly Weir (9)
St Brigid's Primary School, Newmains

My Cold

Colds are red eyes,
Colds are runny noses,
Does anyone want my cold?

Colds aren't super,
Colds aren't splendid,
Does anyone want my cold?

Colds are dreadful,
Colds are awful,
Doesn't anybody want my cold?

Conor Higgins (8)
St Brigid's Primary School, Newmains

Sounds

Birds singing,
Radio blaring,
Mum humming,
    Morning sounds.

Friends chatting,
Children playing,
Boys yelling,
    Playground sounds.

Teacher shouting,
Clock ticking,
Girls drawing,
    Classroom sounds.

Miss Gault talking,
Chairs stacking,
Mouths munching,
    Dinner hall sounds.

Gemma Wilson (8)
St Brigid's Primary School, Newmains

My Cold

Colds are blocked noses,
Colds are high temperatures,
Does anyone want my cold?

Colds aren't pleasant,
Colds aren't nice,
Does anyone want my cold?

Colds are dreadful,
Colds are horrible,
Doesn't anybody want my cold?

Sarah Hamilton (8)
St Brigid's Primary School, Newmains

Sounds

Mum cooking
Dad screaming
Dogs barking
Morning sounds

Bee buzzing
Boys shouting
Children talking
Playground sounds

Thomas and Barry chatting
Girls singing
Games beeping
Classroom sounds

Money rattling
Dinner ladies speaking
Water splashing
Dinner hall sounds!

Barry Gilfillan (8)
St Brigid's Primary School, Newmains

My Cold

Colds are red eyes,
Colds are runny noses,
Does anyone want my cold?

Colds aren't good fun,
Colds aren't wonderful,
Does anyone want my cold?

Colds are nasty,
Colds are awful,
Doesn't anybody want my cold?

Kayleigh Weir (8)
St Brigid's Primary School, Newmains

Sounds

Dad snoring
Kettle boiling
Dogs barking
Morning sounds

Taps running
Bath running
Alarm ringing
Morning sounds

Fridge humming
Tummy rumbling
Toast popping
Morning sounds

Bell ringing
Teacher clapping
Children laughing
Morning over!

Martin Morrow (8)
St Brigid's Primary School, Newmains

My Cold

Colds are bad coughs,
Colds are runny noses,
Does anyone want my cold?

Colds aren't funny,
Colds aren't superb,
Does anyone want my cold?

Colds are awful,
Colds are nasty,
Doesn't anybody want my cold?

A, a, achoo!

Kieran Greig (8)
St Brigid's Primary School, Newmains

Morning Sounds

Beds squeaking,
Dogs barking,
Babies crying,
Morning sounds.

Toilet flushing,
Bath running,
Radiator clunking,
Morning sounds.

Toast popping,
Eggs frying,
Milk pouring,
Morning sounds.

Door banging,
Car revving,
School bell ringing,
Morning over.

Stephen Donnelly (9)
St Brigid's Primary School, Newmains

My Cold

Colds are red eyes,
Colds are throbbing heads,
Does anyone want my cold?

Colds aren't super,
Colds aren't splendid,
Does anyone want my cold?

Colds are awful,
Colds are nasty,
Does anyone want my cold?
Ah ah ahhhh chooo!

Erin McKenna (8)
St Brigid's Primary School, Newmains

I'm Not Feeling Well

Blocked nose,
Red eyes,
Itchy rash,
Feeling sick.

Sore head,
Dead tired,
Red spot,
Feeling sick.

Bad cough,
Cough bottle,
No appetite,
But feeling better.

Eager to play,
Humming quietly,
Jumping about,
Feeling fine!

Nicholas Dow (8)
St Brigid's Primary School, Newmains

My Cold

Colds are red eyes,
Colds are bad coughs,
Does anyone want my cold?

Colds aren't cool,
Colds aren't terrific,
Does anyone want my cold?

Colds are horrid,
Colds are ghastly,
Doesn't anybody want my cold?

Dean Davis (8)
St Brigid's Primary School, Newmains

Alliteration Poem

An amazing, angelic angel
A big brown, bushy brush
A crisp, crunchy cabbage
A dreadful, dusty dictionary
An eager, emerald elf
A fantastic, freaky film
A gorgeous, green gem
A horrifying, hairy horn
An interesting, icy igloo
A jazzy jam jar
A kindly, keen king
A messy, mad magician
A normal, nasty nail
An old, orange ostrich
A pretty, pink pillow
A quaint, quiet queen
A red, rubber rabbit
A spongy, slimy slug
A terrifying toilet troll
An unhappy, ugly unicorn
A very vicious Viking
A weary, watery willow
An exceptional, extraordinary x-ray
A yacky, yellow yeti
A zippy, zappy zebra.

Madeleine Lang (9)
St Brigid's Primary School, Newmains

Alliteration

An amazing, antique amethyst
A big, blue beach ball
A cute, clam, cuddly cat
A delightful, darling daughter
An enormous, energetic elephant
A frozen, funny father
A glamorous, great gentleman
A hopeful, healthy heart
An ideal, imaginative instrument
A jolly, jealous judge
A kind, keen king
A little, laughing lapwing
A mad, muddy monster
A naughty, nasty nestling
An old, orange ostrich
A pure, pink potty
A quick, quarrelsome queen
A round, red ruby
A sad, silly snake
A terrible, terrifying teacher
An unhappy, ugly unicorn
A very, very valuable vase
White, waterproof Wellingtons
An exceptional, extraordinary x-ray
A yucky, yellow yo-yo
A zippy, zappy zebra.

Jamie-Lee Kean (8)
St Brigid's Primary School, Newmains

I'm Not Feeling Well

High temperature,
Thumping head,
Chesty cough,
Feeling sick.

Itchy rash,
Blocked nose,
Red spots,
Feeling sick.

No appetite,
Cosy duvet,
Yucky medicine,
But feeling better.

Bright eyes,
Jumping about,
Rash all gone,
Feeling fine!

Brian Jordan (8)
St Brigid's Primary School, Newmains

Christmas

C hristmas
H aving Christmas dinner with my family
R udolph's nose shining in the sky
 I cicles hanging in from roofs
S anta stuck in the chimney
T oys under the tree
M unching sweets
A t Mass I'm saying my prayers
S anta delivering presents.

Stephen Murray (8)
St Brigid's Primary School, Newmains

I'm Not Feeling Well

Blocked nose,
Throbbing head,
High temperature,
Feeling sick.

Heavy eyes,
Sore cough,
Loud sneezes,
Feeling sick.

Doctor's visit,
Paper hankies,
Cosy duvet,
But feeling better.

Bright eyes,
Clear head,
Hungry again,
Feeling fine!

Stephanie Harbison (9)
St Brigid's Primary School, Newmains

Christmas

C hristmas
H aving a Christmas party
R udolph leading the reindeers
I ce-cold snow on the grass
S anta's sleigh landing on the rooftops
T elling Christmas stories
M ass on Christmas Day
A ll happy for Christmas
S nowmen getting built in the garden.

Thomas Clifford (8)
St Brigid's Primary School, Newmains

I'm Not Feeling Well

Runny eyes,
Sore ears,
Thumping head,
Feeling sick.

Really tired,
Yucky medicine,
Loud sneezes,
Feeling sick.

Doctor's visit,
No appetite,
Cosy duvet,
But feeling better.

Hungry again,
Bright eyes,
Clear head,
Feeling fine.

Dayna Donaldson (8)
St Brigid's Primary School, Newmains

Christmas

C hristmas
H olly hanging on the doors
R eindeer food on the grass
I cy-cold weather
S anta's sleigh bells ringing
T elling Kelly to get to sleep!
M ass on Christmas Day
A sking what time it is?
S o excited about Santa coming.

Emma Weir (8)
St Brigid's Primary School, Newmains

I'm Not Feeling Well

Red eyes,
Sore throat,
Red nose,
Feeling sick.

Bad cough,
Itchy rash,
Sore head,
Feeling sick.

Paper hankies,
Cosy duvet,
Red spots,
But feeling better.

Clear head,
Ready for school,
Jumping on the couch,
Feeling fine!

Aaron Bradshaw (9)
St Brigid's Primary School, Newmains

My Cold

Colds are swollen glands,
Colds are aching shoulders,
Does anyone want my cold?

Colds aren't wonderful,
Colds aren't super,
Does anyone want my cold?

Colds are rotten,
Colds are nasty,
Does anybody want my cold?

Lily Frame (8)
St Brigid's Primary School, Newmains

Morning Sound

Dad snoring,
Dogs Barking,
Birds singing,
Morning sounds.

Mum singing,
Toilet flushing,
Taps running,
Morning sounds.

Dishes washnig,
Sister giggling,
Cereal crunching,
Morning sounds.

Door slamming,
Car engine starting,
School bell ringing,
Morning sounds.

Skye Cutler (8)
St Brigid's Primary School, Newmains

My Cold

Colds are sore throats,
Colds are blocked noses,
Does anyone want my cold?

Colds aren't good fun,
Colds aren't fine,
Does anyone want my cold?

Colds are horrible,
Colds are awful,
Does anybody want my cold?

Declan Lafferty (8)
St Brigid's Primary School, Newmains

My Cold

Colds are red eyes,
Colds are bad coughs,
Does anyone want my cold?

Colds aren't great,
Colds aren't pleasant,
Does anyone want my cold?

Colds are rotten,
Colds are dreadful,
Does anyone want my cold?

Oh!

Diarmiad McGarrell (8)
St Brigid's Primary School, Newmains

My Cold

Colds are red eyes,
Colds are bad coughs,
Does anyone want my cold?

Colds aren't good fun,
Colds aren't cool,
Does anyone want my cold?

Colds are awful,
Cods are rotten,
Doesn't anybody want my cold?

Peter Kirley (8)
St Brigid's Primary School, Newmains

The Super Rocket!

I am a rocket as loud as can be!
I take off like this . . .
5, 4, 3, 2, 1, blast off!
Is there a spaceman inside me?
Yes, there is!
I can remember!
And here I go,
I'm going to land!
It's really fun landing,
When I've landed
The spaceman will get out of me
And then he will go to the space station,
What will he see?

Harry Lindsay (6)
St Margaret's Primary School, Loanhead

The Explosion

I am a rocket
I am in space
I am fast
I am the fastest
Rocket in space
I leave a trail
Of smoke and fire
And loud explosions!

Michael McCormick (6)
St Margaret's Primary School, Loanhead

The Rocket

I am a rocket,
I zoom up in to space,
I fly past the moon,
I see the shiny stars.

Samantha Collier (6)
St Margaret's Primary School, Loanhead

The Spaceman

Here I am
A little spaceman
Zooming off into space
I can see so many different planets
They are all nice
Especially Uranus
All the colours
Blend in together
Blue, green
And milky-white.

Clare Phillips (6)
St Margaret's Primary School, Loanhead

The North Star

I am the North Star
I can see
Planets and the dark sky
I can feel
Brightness
I can hear
Silence.

Eilidh Joyce (6)
St Margaret's Primary School, Loanhead

The West Star

I am the west star
I am high above the Earth
I can see the big moon
I can see high above
I feel happy and sparkly.

Daniel Turner (7)
St Margaret's Primary School, Loanhead

The Ball Of Fire

I am a ball of fire
I am hot like
Boiling water
I look down
And I see nothing
But emptiness
All around me
I feel lonely
I want to be
A shooting star with friends.

Lauren Dalgetty (7)
St Margaret's Primary School, Loanhead

The Shooting Star

I am the shooting star,
I can see all the planets,
They all shine,
A bit like the sun,
I feel so powerful
That I go so fast,
I am also
Beautiful.

Marie Barry (7)
St Margaret's Primary School, Loanhead

I Am An Astronaut

I am an astronaut,
I can see dazzling stars through the dark sky,
I can feel dust slipping through my hands,
I can hear silence through the dark night sky,
I feel terrific.

Karen Zhu (7)
St Margaret's Primary School, Loanhead

The Rocket

I am a rocket,
I am lifting off to Mars,
I can get there in 2 minutes,
I am the fastest rocket in space.
I am on Mars,
It is really red,
I can see lots of stars,
I can also see the moon,
It is fun.

Lewis Brown (6)
St Margaret's Primary School, Loanhead

The Milky Way

I am the Milky Way
I can hear nothing but silence
I look beautiful
I am surrounded by planets
The planets are much darker than me
I look beautiful because of my colours
I am blue and green and silvery white.

Chloe Coombs (7)
St Margaret's Primary School, Loanhead

Shock!

Shock is as black as a cave.
Shock is like going through the woods.
Shock feels like being scared like a man with an axe.
Shock is like a crunched up face.
Shock smells like a poisonous word.
Don't get a *shock!*

Theo Koulis (7)
St Margaret's Primary School, Loanhead

Sadness

Sadness is dark blue like paint in the darkness.
Sadness looks small like tiny teardrops of rain
Falling from the sky.
Sadness sounds like a door screeching
In an old castle.
Sadness smells like horrid onions making you cry.
Sadness feels like everything is sinking
In sad sinking sand.
Sadness tastes like a drip of water in your mouth
Which falls from your eyes.
Sadness reminds me of when I cry.

Eilidh Ramsay (9)
St Margaret's Primary School, Loanhead

Excitement

Excitement is bright pink like candyfloss in my mouth.
Excitement looks like ten smiling teddies all in a row.
Excitement is like loud, happy beating in your heart.
Excitement smells like perfume that is bright purple.
Excitement feels like a brass band thumping on your heart.
Excitement tastes like a lollipop on my tongue.
Excitement reminds me of the day Jesus opened the gates of Heaven.

Lyndsay Turner (9)
St Margaret's Primary School, Loanhead

Anger

Anger is black like the dark night sky.
Anger looks horrible like a tipped over rubbish bin.
Anger sounds nasty like a screaming rat.
Anger smells disgusting like rotten eggs.
Anger feels spiky like a hedgehog.
Anger tastes toxic like a poisonous spider.
Anger reminds me of a red screwed-up face.

Naa Shika Tetteh-Lartey (9)
St Margaret's Primary School, Loanhead

Angry Mars

If I were Mars
I would have anger inside me.
I would look red and frightening.
I would see little stars clear in the sky,
I would feel like I could burst them all.
I would shoot all the comets
And shooting stars.
I would be able to see all the planets,
I would *roar* at them!

Katelyn Grant (7)
St Margaret's Primary School, Loanhead

Happiness

Happiness tastes as sweet as a strawberry.
Happiness looks like Heaven above.
Happiness sounds like laughter.
Happiness is bright pink like candyfloss.
Happiness smells like a petal from a rose.
Happiness feels like the wind in the trees.
That is the poem of happiness.

Indya Nisbet (7)
St Margaret's Primary School, Loanhead

Anger

Anger is red like a zooming volcano.
Anger looks like a very mean face.
Anger sounds like burning fire.
Anger smells like poisonous paint.
Anger feels horrible like a leaping frog.
Anger tastes disgusting like worms.
Anger reminds me of when I get in a row.

Tanisha Buerle (7)
St Margaret's Primary School, Loanhead

Anger

Anger is red like horror,
It looks like someone has just eaten a strong strawberry.
Anger sounds like someone shouting and charging.
Anger smells like a red-hot, burnt pie.
Anger feels like horrible, soggy bread.
Anger tastes like flames.
Anger reminds me of myself.

Sheryl Cochrane (8)
St Margaret's Primary School, Loanhead

Shock

Shock is silver like a glistening sword.
Shock looks bright like lightning flashing.
Shock sounds loud like a big ship crashing into rocks.
Shock smells like a candle going out in the darkness.
Shock feels strong like a powerful wind at its best.
Shock tastes smooth like water from the tap.
Shock reminds me of when I got my picture taken.

John Weir (8)
St Margaret's Primary School, Loanhead

Happiness

Happiness tastes like chocolate Roses melting in my mouth.
Happiness sounds like a bird singing in a tree
On a bright summer's morning.
Happiness smells like a sunflower just bloomed.
Happiness feels like dancing softly in my heart.
Happiness looks like my little sister fast asleep thinking of playmates.

Yasmin Crosbie (8)
St Margaret's Primary School, Loanhead

Darkness

Darkness looks like a slime dripping Grim Reaper.
Darkness sounds like a loud, shrieking scream.
Darkness tastes like rotten eggs slapped on mouldy bread.
Darkness smells like the stench of a cave when you walk in.
Darkness feels like a knife driving right through your wrist.
Darkness reminds me of the shapes in a dark room
That look like they're going to kill you.

Robbie Forbes (11)
St Margaret's Primary School, Loanhead

Anger

Anger sounds like an extremely loud exploding volcano.
Anger smells like blazing, burning black smoke.
Anger tastes like a ripping rough stab in the back.
Anger reminds me of a stabbing attack.
Anger feels like your head has got to pop.
Anger looks red like when you kill someone and leave blood.

Lewis Crosbie (10)
St Margaret's Primary School, Loanhead

Love

Love looks like a beating heart.
Love sounds like music to my ears.
Love tastes like the sweet sensation of chocolate.
Love smells like the sweet smell of babies.
Love feels tickily inside.
Love reminds me of fireworks and stars.

Brooke McGuinness (11)
St Margaret's Primary School, Loanhead

Fear

Fear is as black as the night sky in November.
Fear looks like a shadow in an abandoned town.
If fear was a person it wouldn't make a sound.
Fear sounds like footsteps in an empty castle.
If you could taste fear it would taste like toxic waste.
And if I could feel fear it would feel like ice.
If you met fear and if fear met you,
Both of you would scream *arrgggghhhh.*

Paul Darcy (8)
St Margaret's Primary School, Loanhead

Fear

Fear is white like the moon at midnight.
Fear looks thin like a 2D man on his side.
Fear sounds like a bow scraping a violin.
Fear smells cold and dark like icy-cold water.
Fear feels like a spike ball.
Fear tastes horrible like a rotten apple.
Fear reminds me of falling off the stairs into nothing.

Benjamin Aarhus (9)
St Margaret's Primary School, Loanhead

Anger

Anger looks like a volcano erupting.
Anger sounds like a roaring, raging fire.
Anger tastes like fire balls in your mouth.
Anger smells like molten lava.
Anger feels like a crown of thorns on your head.
Anger reminds me of everything.

William Anderson (10)
St Margaret's Primary School, Loanhead

Fear

Fear is pale like a piece of paper.
Fear looks like wide open eyes.
Fear sounds like someone screaming.
Fear smells like poison.
Fear tastes like slimy frogs' legs.
Fear touches like a skeleton's hand.
Fear reminds me of my dad when he is angry with me.
That's why you don't want to *fear*.

Emily Dalgetty (7)
St Margaret's Primary School, Loanhead

Happiness

Happiness is like a wonderful wedding in the spring.
Happiness sounds like the newborn cries of kittens.
Happiness tastes like toffee ripple ice cream.
Happiness smells like fabric softener on my clothes.
Happiness seems like another day at school.
Happiness feels like playing football.
Happiness reminds me of a flying kestrel soaring through the sky.

Raymond Brumby (12)
St Margaret's Primary School, Loanhead

Fear

Fear is white like the clouds.
Fear looks nervous like me.
Fear sounds frightening like a child screaming.
Fear smells sweaty like someone playing basketball.

Simon McCormick (9)
St Margaret's Primary School, Loanhead

Fear

Fear is like a dead bleeding rose in a graveyard.
Fear smells like being buried beside a dead man.
Fear sounds like the screeching of a bat as it is killing you.
Fear feels like being eaten by a lion bit by bit.
Fear tastes like mud splatted on blood.
Fear reminds me of looking in a dead man's eyes as he
walked around.

Ryan Crosbie (12)
St Margaret's Primary School, Loanhead

Beachcombing

On Monday it was sunny and warm
Went to the beach and cut my foot on barnacles

On Tuesday it was a bit windy
I found a rusty old jacket and threw it away

On Wednesday, a summer's day
I saw a dead seal covered in beasties
Left it alone

On Thursday it was a good day
I found nothing
Just a big lump of sand

On Friday it was a hot day
I saw a lobster and it nipped my finger

On Saturday I found a broken old shoe
It was no good for me 'cause it was covered in sand

On Sunday I went fishing
And found a dead flatfish
I picked it up and threw it back in the water.

Chelsea Meadows (10)
Sandhaven Primary School, Sandhaven

The Beachcomber

On Monday I found an oil drum, I didn't really want it
So I flung it into the air.
On Tuesday I found a shell, I put it next to my ear
And something clipped me hard, it must have been a crab.
On Wednesday I found a bit of wood from a fence,
I used it in the fire, well, at least I can stay dry if it rains.
On Thursday I found a lobster, I cooked it for my tea,
It was nice, but when I found it, it nearly pinched me.
On Friday I found a shoe, it wasn't much use because it didn't fit me,
The shoe even had a big hole in it.
On Saturday I found a flatfish called a sole,
It was kind of hard to catch because it was really fast,
I kept it as a pet and my mum told me what it ate.
On Sunday I found a can with an eel and a fish inside,
I put them back in the sea because I know they will die out of water,
A few minutes later, it started to rain,
Good job I had my raincoat like my mum said.

Kyle Davis (10)
Sandhaven Primary School, Sandhaven

Beach

On Monday it was sunny
And I found maggots crawling up a rock.
On Tuesday I found a whale's bone
On the golden sand.
On Wednesday I found a hat
Sailing on the silver sea.
On Thursday my dog found a ragged
Old ripped salty boot.
On Friday I found the dead body
Of a seal with flies scuttling on it.
On Saturday me and my friends
Found a seal's bone on the silver lining of the sea.
On Sunday I found a great big dollop of seaweed
So I gave it back to the sea.

Stephanie Smith (10)
Sandhaven Primary School, Sandhaven

The Beachcomber

Monday it was a bit breezy
And I found a jacket
It was green and yellow
But it was too small

On Tuesday the weather was getting better
So I found a frayed, old rope
To tie toys together with

Wednesday's weather was better
And I found a whole load of seaweed
That you could eat if you liked it

On Thursday it got warmer
And I found a top hat
But it was ripped and torn

Friday it was warm
And I found a load of shells
They were beautiful
So I took them home

On Saturday it was really hot
I found two boots
But they were both different
So that's not useful

Sunday it was boiling
I found a box of treasure
And that was useful
But I noticed I was only dreaming.

Megan Beedie (10)
Sandhaven Primary School, Sandhaven

Beachcombing

Monday I found a boot
All torn up
So I put it in the bin

Tuesday I saw a rope
Frayed at the bottom
I put it in the sea

Wednesday it was windy
A plastic bag blown in the wind
Blown from a boat out at sea

Thursday, a beautiful day
Too nice to go beachcombing
I slid down the sand dunes instead

Friday I collected shells
Mussels, limpets, clams
Took them home for my collection

Saturday I stepped on maggots
Wiggling beside a dead eel
Licking my toes

Sunday it was raining
So I stayed at home
Dreaming about finding gold.

Jason Milne (10)
Sandhaven Primary School, Sandhaven

The Beachcomber

On Monday it was sunny
I went beachcombing and found a crab
It almost bit me on the tummy
On Tuesday I found a dead seal
The seal smelt really bad
And then I saw an unusual-looking eel
On Wednesday I found a bone
It looked very interesting
Because beside it was a comb
On Thursday I found a sole
It is a kind of flatfish
And then something caught my eye
It was a long pole
On Friday I found a hat
It wasn't any use to me
But then I saw a rotten old rat
On Saturday I found a glove
It must have come from a fisherman
Then I heard a noise, it was a seagull up above
On Sunday I found a sheep's skull
It was very fascinating
Then I dreamed of a pot of gold!

Jade Davis (11)
Sandhaven Primary School, Sandhaven

Beachcombing

On Monday it was warm
I found a blue oil drum
It was in good condition
On Tuesday it was sunny
I found an old shoe
It wasn't any use to me
On Wednesday it was a lovely day
The only problem was
The harbour was bare
On Thursday it was hot
I found a dark black lobster
It was rotten so I never took it home
On Friday it was dull
I only found a seal's skull
I never liked the look of it
On Saturday it was warm
So I walked down to the harbour
The only thing I saw was some seagulls flying above me
On Sunday it was sunny
I found a net
I saw fish in it
So I just walked home and left it alone.

Heather Stewart (11)
Sandhaven Primary School, Sandhaven

Beachcombing

Monday - warm and sunny
I found a DVD
When I got home it didn't work, so I threw it away

Tuesday - quite cold
I found a flower ornament, which was a bit broken
When I got back, I gave it to my mum and dad

Wednesday - hot and sunny
I found a jacket
When I got home it was no use because it didn't fit

Thursday - quite hot
I found a big shiny shell
When I got home I gave it to my granny

Friday - really hot
I found my favourite book
But when I got it home, it was torn

Saturday - sunny, but a bit cold
I found a big blue whale
But it was dead

Sunday - hot
I found a necklace
When I got home my mum said I could keep it.

Skye Thompson (11)
Sandhaven Primary School, Sandhaven

Beachcombing

Monday - hot summer's day
I found a plastic bottle, not much I could do with it
So I threw it away

Tuesday - a really windy day
I caught a big lobster black and blue colour
Took it home, cooked it and I ate it

Wednesday - perfect day
Found a dead crab, really big, orange-red colour
Gave it to my dad and he ate it

Thursday - really warm day
I found some limpets - used it for bait and caught a mackerel
Didn't want it, so I put it back

Friday - really sunny day
I caught an eel and I didn't want it
So I gave it to my granda and he kept it in a bucket

Saturday - brilliant day
Got my fishing rod, but never caught anything
So I went back home

Sunday - hot day
Went fishing, but the scurries were annoying me
So I went to my friend's.

Martin-Andrew Duncan (10)
Sandhaven Primary School, Sandhaven

Beachcombing

Monday
Summer's day, really hot
Found some thick wood
Tuesday
The sun is shining
I saw some shiny shells
Wednesday
The sky is blue
Found some broken bottles
Thursday
A bit of wind
I saw some scrawny feathers
Friday
Lovely sunny day
Found a hat with a pom-pom
Saturday
A bit of grey in the sky
I saw some cracked shells
Sunday
A warm day
I found a plastic bag.

Caroline Russell (11)
Sandhaven Primary School, Sandhaven

The Beachcomber

On Monday I found ropes from a fisherman's net.
On Tuesday I found a dead seal with maggots - which I left.
On Wednesday I found a boot - all torn and ripped, I flung it back.
On Thursday I found some dark black bladder wrack.
On Friday I found nothing but sun.
On Saturday I saw a huge sea urchin.
On Sunday I found splintered planks of wood.

Keir Allan (10)
Sandhaven Primary School, Sandhaven

Beachcombing

Monday I found a tyre
All rusty and dirty
I cleaned it up and made a swing
Tuesday I saw a bottle
A bottle with a note
I wonder if it was a treasure map?
Wednesday it was breezy
I saw a rope
It was dusty and sandy
Thursday a blue-black lobster
Caught in a creel
I cooked it and shared it with my family
Friday bladder wrack seaweed
Black, slimy and wet
I left it where it was.

Johnathan Beedie (10)
Sandhaven Primary School, Sandhaven

Beachcombing

On Monday it was sunny and hot
I went to the beach and found a plastic bag
On Tuesday I went to the beach
And found a bone
On Wednesday it was hot
So I went to the beach and found a stick
On Thursday I went to the beach
And caught a crab under a stone
On Friday it was a sunny and hot day
I found a spider crab at the beach under a dead seal
On Saturday I went to the beach
And I found a trainer, it was very soggy
On Sunday it was very hot
So I went to the beach for a swim and I found a chair.

Andrew Smith (10)
Sandhaven Primary School, Sandhaven

Beachcombing

On Monday it was sunny with a breeze
I found some pieces of China with beautiful patterns
And some pieces of glass.

On Tuesday I found a feather from a seagull,
But it blew out of my hand,
I found a piece of interesting wood with the name 'Prancing Star'.

On Wednesday it was cold and drizzly,
So I was wrapped up warm,
I found a shell and it was moving - a hermit crab.

On Thursday I found nothing because it was snowing,
The ground was so white and I was so disappointed.

On Friday I found some slates, but nothing else,
It was pouring, it was so cold,
I just threw the slates back in the water.

On Saturday it was windy so I just sat on a rock
And looked at the sea,
The sea was raging, I saw a seal sitting on a rock.

On Sunday it was so sunny,
I found some beautiful shells,
Purple ones, blue ones and silver ones too,
I found them in the glistening golden sand,
I felt so warm and happy.

Terri-Lee Batty (11)
Sandhaven Primary School, Sandhaven